ALSO BY BEN SHAPIRO

The Authoritarian Movement
How to Destroy America in Three Easy Steps
The Right Side of History
Bullies
Say It's So
True Allegiance
The People vs. Barrack Obama
Primetime Propaganda
Project President
Porn Generation
Brainwashed

LIONS AND SCAVENGERS

THE TRUE STORY OF AMERICA (AND HER CRITICS)

BEN SHAPIRO

#1 *New York Times* Bestselling Author

THRESHOLD EDITIONS
New York   Amsterdam/Antwerp   London
Toronto   Sydney/Melbourne   New Delhi

Threshold Editions
An Imprint of Simon & Schuster, LLC
1230 Avenue of the Americas
New York, NY 10020

For more than 100 years, Simon & Schuster has championed authors and the stories they create. By respecting the copyright of an author's intellectual property, you enable Simon & Schuster and the author to continue publishing exceptional books for years to come. We thank you for supporting the author's copyright by purchasing an authorized edition of this book.

No amount of this book may be reproduced or stored in any format, nor may it be uploaded to any website, database, language-learning model, or other repository, retrieval, or artificial intelligence system without express permission. All rights reserved. Inquiries may be directed to Simon & Schuster, 1230 Avenue of the Americas, New York, NY 10020 or permissions@simonandschuster.com.

Copyright © 2025 by Ben Shapiro

All rights reserved, including the right to reproduce this book or portions thereof in any form whatsoever. For information, address Threshold Editions Subsidiary Rights Department, 1230 Avenue of the Americas, New York, NY 10020.

First Threshold Editions hardcover edition September 2025

THRESHOLD EDITIONS and colophon are trademarks of Simon & Schuster, LLC

Simon & Schuster strongly believes in freedom of expression and stands against censorship in all its forms. For more information, visit BooksBelong.com.

For information about special discounts for bulk purchases, please contact Simon & Schuster Special Sales at 1-866-506-1949 or business@simonandschuster.com.

The Simon & Schuster Speakers Bureau can bring authors to your live event. For more information or to book an event, contact the Simon & Schuster Speakers Bureau at 1-866-248-3049 or visit our website at www.simonspeakers.com.

Interior design by Jaime Putorti

Manufactured in the United States of America

10 9 8 7 6 5 4 3 2 1

Library of Congress Control Number is available.

ISBN 978-1-6680-9788-5
ISBN 978-1-6680-9790-8 (ebook)

To the Lions—the Hunters, Warriors and Weavers—who build, defend, and maintain the greatest civilization in the history of mankind against the Scavengers who would destroy that civilization from within.

CONTENTS

Introduction	1
Chapter One: The Way of the Lion	13
Chapter Two: The Pride	27
Chapter Three: The Rules of the Pride	55
Chapter Four: The Way of the Scavenger	93
Chapter Five: The Pack	123
Chapter Six: The Rules of the Pack	157
Chapter Seven: Bloodlust and Bloodguilt	191
Chapter Eight: The Lion Roars	217
Acknowledgments	229
Notes	233

LIONS
AND
SCAVENGERS

INTRODUCTION

LONDON, ENGLAND

A tension lies at the core of our being.
 It roils us. It churns our guts. It boils our brains.
 That tension lies between two opposing forces.
 Those forces beat within every man's breast. They fight for supremacy within every civilization. One must triumph, and one must fall.
 The spirit of the Lion.
 The spirit of the Scavenger.

I write these words in London, England.

I write them in disappointment and horror and dismay.

For London has been conquered by the Scavengers.

Just last weekend, London saw a massive river of protesters, hundreds of thousands strong, marching, their banners unfurled: the banners of terrorist groups and of communists and of transgender activists, gathered together to revolt against the civilization that has given them their rights and their prosperity and their power. These marchers have gathered to protest in favor of the terror group Hamas; it has been just a few weeks since the slaughter of 1,200 Jews and kidnapping of 250 others on October 7, 2023, in the envelope surrounding the Gaza Strip. Members of Hamas and Palestinian civilians flooded into villages, a music festival, homes; they dragged out men, women, and children. They livestreamed their crimes.

And the Scavengers have risen in rage—in support of Hamas. As the savagery—mass murder, rape, and kidnapping—took place, one commentator posted on social media, "what did y'all think decolonization meant? vibes? papers? essays? Losers."[1] Her comment received nearly 100,000 likes. And it spoke to the very core of the Scavengers: All inhumanity against the Lions is justified.

And so the Scavengers have gathered, here in the beating heart of what was once the center of Western civilization, to bay for more blood, and to scream at a West that insists that defense against terror is the first right of all men.

They march with their red flags held high, ecstatically singing the praises of murderers and rapists—for this is their opportunity to castigate the Pride, to bring it low. The British Communist Party issued a statement in solidarity with Hamas, condemning the Israeli government on the *day after October 7*, before Israeli military action had even begun. Jeremy Corbyn, former leader of the Labor Party, appeared at rallies flanked by Palestinian flags. The hilariously bizarre group "Queers for Palestine" quickly formed, in solidarity with people who would throw queers off buildings at the first available opportunity if given half a chance. Many of the most ardent libertines have thrown their support behind Hamas, claiming solidarity with those who would throw them off roofs at the first opportunity.

Anything to tear down the Pride.

This is not mere anti-Semitism. Anti-Semitism is an age-old hatred rooted in a conspiracy theory; it takes many forms and has countless victims.

This is something different. It is a united, coalitional hatred of the West.

In *The Lord of the Rings*, J. R. R. Tolkien wrote of the hordes of Mordor—stand-ins for the Nazis and their allies, by way of metaphor—gathering on the plains outside the gates of Minas Tirith, the last redoubt of mankind:

> The plain was dark with their marching companies, and as far as eyes could strain in the mirk there sprouted, like a foul fungus-growth, all about the beleaguered city great camps of tents, black or sombre red ... All day the labour went forward, while the men of Minas Tirith looked on, unable to hinder it.[2]

So it goes today, in London.

The marchers march.

Their numbers increase.

And the Scavengers cast their avaricious, ravenous eyes across the landscape ... and see no one to oppose them.

The Lions are gone.

And without the spirit of the Lion, our civilization collapses.

What is the spirit of the Lion?

The spirit of success. Of responsibility. Of duty.

The Lion understands that the universe is constructed by a set of rules he can discern; he thrills in his capacity to choose, knowing that it lifts him above beasts; he embraces his moral duties in the world, revels in his responsibilities.

The Lion comes in many types.

The Lion is a Hunter: creative, audacious, innovative. He bends the world to his will; he forges new paths and crafts new solutions. When faced with a problem, the Lion does not complain about the unfairness of life: He seeks an answer. The Lion is bold and persistent. Failure does not unnerve him—it teaches him. The Lion knows that boldness of purpose and willingness to undergo risk are the driving forces of any successful civilization. He believes in the words of Proverbs: "Where there is no vision, the people perish."[3]

The Lion is a warrior: He is steadfast in defending himself, his family, and his culture. He understands that the spirit of the Scavenger is always abroad, and that only strength can defend against it. The Lion knows that the universe was created dangerous—and that courage and steadfastness in the face of risk is the only proper response. The Lion lives by the words of C. S. Lewis:

> [C]ourage is not simply one of the virtues, but the form of every virtue at the testing point, which means, at the point of highest reality. A chastity or honesty, or mercy, which yields to danger will be chaste or honest or merciful only on conditions.[4]

And the Lion is a weaver: He is prudent, merciful, and strong, dedicated to the construction and maintenance of the social fabric, the ties that bind. The Lion weaves together the disparate strands of family and society, and holds them together with love and prudence. They often go unnoticed and uncelebrated, but the weavers are the true heroes of our civilization. The weaver lives out the credo of Seneca:

It is a sacrilege to harm your country; it is therefore sacrilege to harm a citizen, too (for he is a part of your country—and its parts will be sacred, if the whole commands veneration); and therefore it will be a sacrilege to harm even a human being, since he is a citizen in that greater city of yours.[5]

Together, the hunters, warriors, and weavers form a Pride.

That Pride is governed by rules—rules that ensure the flourishing of a community and a civilization. The Lions know that within them, the spirit of the Scavenger still lurks—and so the Pride constructs a system of rules.

Those rules protect individual rights and foster public virtue.

They replenish and reinvigorate the spirit of the Lions that comprise it.

If Lions fall, so does the Pride; if the Pride falls, so do the Lions.

A Pride of Lions can accomplish nearly anything.

Unless the Pride falls to the Pack.

To the spirit of the Scavenger.

The spirit of the Scavenger is the spirit of envy.

That spirit animates those who destroy successful men and civilizations.

The Scavenger is driven by a burning impulse: the impulse to escape his own failures and shortcomings by blaming others. The Scavenger believes that his own failure is the fault of the stars, of the fates . . . but mostly, of the Lion.

The Scavenger is a creature of frustration, alienation, and vengeance.

The Scavenger does not believe in an understandable universe in which success is the result of performance of duty; instead, the Scavenger believes that any such argument is a guise for power, and power alone. The Scavenger, in his perverse projection, believes that there is a Great Conspiracy against him—and that the only path to success lies in tearing away at that Great Conspiracy, with tooth and with claw. The Scavenger lives by the credo of Satan in John Milton's *Paradise Lost*: "Better to reign in Hell, than serve in Heav'n."[6]

And how many Hells on earth have the Scavengers created!

The Scavenger comes in many forms, too.

The Scavenger is a Looter: greedy, jealous, and violent. He claims the innovation and work of others as his birthright. He sees those who are productive—and who are therefore successful—as oppressors, and himself as a member of the oppressed. The only way, the Looter believes, to free himself of his shackles is to wreck the very systems that allow for innovation and productivity. The Looter has no qualms about utilizing violence to seize the means of production, to bleed the Hunter dry, to crush him beneath the grinding gears of a great, hideous machine. The Looter relies on the Great Conspiracy to justify himself. He lives by the mantra of Mao Zedong: "Political power grows out of the barrel of a gun."[7]

The Scavenger is a Lecher: rebellious, perverse, and leering. The Lecher believes that his own alienation from society—and his consequent failure of soul—is the fault of a system shot through with false piety. The Lecher understands that perhaps the strongest human drive—lust—can be weaponized against the Lion and the Pride. The Lecher believes that his own fulfillment will arise from the destruction of those very systems of morality that undergird a thriving social fabric—that he can only be free when all of society embraces the perverse at the expense of the virtuous.

And the Scavenger is a Barbarian: jealous, enraged, and violent.

The Barbarian is an outsider to Western civilization who believes that all of his own maladies and ills can be laid at the feet of the "colonizers" of the West. In fact, the Barbarian argues, only violence against his purported victimizers can free him of the servile mentality that these very colonizers have instilled in him. The Barbarian speaks in the language of mass-murdering communist monster Che Guevara, whose visage still graces the T-shirts of thousands of misbegotten American college students, championing the power of hatred: "hatred as an element of struggle; unbending hatred for the enemy, which pushes a human being beyond his natural limitations, making him into an effective, violent, selective, and cold-blooded killing machine."[8]

Together, the Looters, Lechers, and Barbarians form a Pack.

At first, the Pack forms in opposition to the Pride: It forms a coalition, mottled and kaleidoscopic, ever changing in its internal power dynamics, but rigid in its orientation against the Pride. The Pack exists to overthrow the existing order; only later do the survivors learn the horrors to which they will be subjected. Those horrors come in many forms, but they all add up to one universal truth: human suffering.

If the Pack triumphs, everyone pays the price.

The fall of London is symptomatic not merely of the growing power of the Pack.

It is a symptom of a civilization that has lost the courage of its convictions.

Any civilization that loses its confidence opens itself to predations from those who would tear it down, from within and without. Lions build civilizations. Those Lions must maintain constant vigilance, never-ending deterrence, eternal strength. If they weaken, the Scavengers attack.

The Scavengers gather at the gates, waiting for any sign of vulnerability.

The gates must be bolstered. For once a crack appears, it quickly becomes a breach.

That external threat will become matched by an internal one.

Lions must pass on their ways to their children. They must teach their traditions, their purpose, their roles. They must instill their values and then demand virility.

For if we all have two impulses beating within us—the Spirit of the Lion and the Spirit of the Scavenger, vying for supremacy—then the failure of the Lions is the success of the Scavenger.

If the Lions fail their children, their own children *join the Scavengers*. Unmoored from a civilization their parents refuse to defend, they become rabid, and go in search of revenge on those who left them adrift. They lead a rebellion of privilege: Bred into unearned prosperity, but taught ignorance and dependency, they look close at hand for monsters to destroy.

They become the hellish mutation of a spent culture.

The children of Lions can *become* Scavengers.

The civilizational Lions—if they give up their virility for cowardice or timidity—collapse before the frenzied mob of their children. Enraged at the churches their parents abandoned, incensed at the free-market system that handed them wealth they never earned, livid at the men and women who defend the very countries and towns they inhabit, a generation of newly-turned Scavengers now threatens civilization from within. They *open* the gates. They welcome in their fellow Scavengers.

And the Scavengers run amok.

The West was warned, of course.

In 1897, Rudyard Kipling wrote a poem for the Diamond Jubilee of Queen Victoria. The British Empire was still at its height, but Kipling wrote a warning to his civilization, a warning that they must not, for a moment, forget the values that had animated them and brought them here:

The tumult and the shouting dies;
The Captains and the Kings depart:
Still stands Thine ancient sacrifice,
An humble and a contrite heart.
Lord God of Hosts, be with us yet,
Lest we forget—lest we forget.[9]

Yet the British did forget. Abandoning the values of their ancestors, wooed by the promise of a postcivilizational welfare utopia, Britain slipped into her dotage. Edmund Burke warned of the temptations of a vast welfare state designed to ameliorate complaints at the cost of dynamism, innovation, and self-reliance in 1795, lamenting any system in which governments "attempt to feed the people out of the hands of the magistrates":

If once they are habituated to it, though but for one half-year, they will never be satisfied to have it otherwise. And having looked to government for bread, on the very first scarcity they will turn and bite the hand that fed them. To avoid that evil, government will redouble the causes of it; and then it will become inveterate and incurable.

The warning went unheeded. In the post–World War II era, Great Britain turned inward in shame and exhaustion, away from both her empire and her principles, in search of a sterile redistributionism. Robbed of its initiative, a civilization of Lions turned toward senility. In 1969, poet Philip Larkin pointedly described the new malaise of his civilization:

> *Next year we shall be living in a country*
> *That brought its soldiers home for lack of money.*
> *The statues will be standing in the same*
> *Tree-muffled squares, and look nearly the same.*
> *Our children will not know it's a different country.*
> *All we can hope to leave them now is money.*

Yet even that hope has gone unfulfilled. The Scavengers never rested. They never surrendered. They never stopped. They sought entry.

And they found willing allies within.

As it turns out, the beneficiaries of a managed and sterile civilization are not grateful for what they have been given. They turn on it with snarling fury. All of this was predicted by George Orwell in 1940, when he wrote of why young Europeans had turned to Hitler:

> Whereas Socialism, and even capitalism in a grudging way, have said to people "I offer you a good time," Hitler has said to them "I offer you struggle, danger and death," and as a result a whole nation flings itself at his feet.

Yesterday, they marched with Hitler.

Today, they march with Hamas.

The world continues to spin, but human nature does not change.

And so Britain has been remade, from without and within. The gates were opened by the children of the Lions; the Scavengers storm the streets of London together. They stand together, hundreds of thousands strong, waving the flags of the enemies of our civilization, tearing down those old statues from the tree-muffled squares.

Despite what Larkin wrote, the children certainly know it's a different country.

And so here we are.

In London.

The shadows grow long.

The darkness encroaches.

The monuments of our past stand covered in the graffiti of terror supporters, communists, and lechers. The streets are filled with the stench of civilizational decay.

Innocents fear to go about at night.

Predators do not.

The Lions move slowly, their limbs weary, their breath labored.
They are vulnerable.
The Scavengers lurk in the shadows
They gather in the darkness.
And then they attack.
One by one, they kill off the Lions—the Lions who are too tired to fight, too divided to unite, too old to roar.
Soon, very soon, the scavengers will master the world.
Unless.

CHAPTER ONE

THE WAY OF THE LION

ROME, ITALY

You can feel the ghosts.

And they stir.

Italy is one of the most beautiful countries on the planet. And Rome is a treasure chest of a city. It is a city of layers: layers of history piled atop one another, a glorious and haunting archaeological tell that serves as a living city. Stroll past the Roman Colosseum, where Christians were fed to lions; under the Arch of Titus, where the Roman emperor commemorated his destruction of the city of Jerusalem; and toward St. Peter's Basilica, where Michelangelo's heartbreaking sculpture of a Jewish mother cradling the body of her sacrificed son still brings you to tears, centuries later.

And then make your way toward the Sistine Chapel.

The ceiling of the Sistine Chapel was controversial in its time. Now it has become so well-known that you would expect it to feel kitschy and overplayed.

Instead, in an age in which we have forgotten the voices of our ghosts, it speaks.

The depiction of God—that muscled Old Man in the sky—reaching down to Adam, the first man made in His image; the finger of the Divine, nearly touching the finger of man, passing into him the power of creation, the unique power of man to shape the world in which he lives; the knowledge that with that power comes both risk and opportunity. That gap between the fingers of God and Adam—some three-quarters of an inch—reminds us that while man is made in God's image, he can never reach God's perfection, and that man's understanding and God's remain forever separate.

The Creation of Man lies at the root of our civilization.

For in creating man, God gave him both power and responsibility.

On this day, we are taping in the ruins of Ostia.

Our company, *The Daily Wire*, has commissioned a series on the ideas and history of Western civilization, starring Jordan Peterson. Jordan has taped with me in ancient Jerusalem; with religious symbolist Jonathan Pageau on the Via Dolorosa; with philosophy scholar Spencer Klavan in Athens; and with Bishop Robert Barron in Rome.

Today we are to sit together and speak about the big ideas of the West: the things that make the West unique. The history of the city goes back centuries before the birth of Christ; the ruins that can be viewed today date back to the third century BC. Ostia became a vital port for the Roman republic. But Ostia became most famous for her part in the religious awakening of St. Augustine. In his *Confessions*, Augustine writes of speaking with his mother near the day of her death, in a garden in Ostia, probably within sight of where we now talk. Nearly two millennia later, we are in the city of Augustine, separated only by the passing breath of time.

It is cool as the sunlight diminishes; in the quiet of the burgeoning evening, we discuss the value of revealed religion and Greek reason, of ritual and ideal, of the communal and the individual. Citations of Aristotle and Augustine and Maimonides and Kant fill the round. It's exciting and wonderful and joyous. It makes me think of the Socratic notion that a good afterlife lies in an eternal search for "true and false knowledge; as in this world, so also in the next."

The arena is empty, but the voices reverberate.

These are ideas that *feel* new, even though they have been put aside or forgotten in favor of glib existentialism or ironic nihilism or resigned determinism. These are the ideas that formed the civilization that brought us everything from private property to the moon landing, everything from democracy to modern medicine.

These are ideas with *meaning*.

As the sun sets, we walk back to our cars, thinking about the ideas that have animated a civilization. Later we'll meet up for dinner, talk about those ideas long into the evening.

But as we walk back to our cars, the site is quiet.

We all feel the weight of Western civilization. Rome and Greece and Jerusalem and London and Washington; Tours and Lepanto and Vienna; the profane and the holy, the violence and the peace, the bank and the cathedral—you can feel them all.

Mostly what you feel is the ghosts.

The ghosts of the Lions.

And they stir.

PHILOSOPHY OF THE LION

Lions have a philosophy—a deceptively simple one.

Often, it is not held as a philosophy, but rather as a way of life. Few Lions spend time thinking about the deep roots of their actions in the world. They act in the world as Lions, confidently and without compromise or apology. Ask them their philosophy, and they may laugh at you—they know, deep in their bones, what it is they believe, even if they cannot articulate it.

It does not take a philosopher to be a Lion.

Yet Lions *do* have an unstated, implicit philosophy, a set of principles by which they live. It is a philosophy developed over the ages, handed down father to son and mother to daughter, a chain of teaching stretching back thousands of years. That philosophy can be summed up in the contrast and symbiosis between Jerusalem and Athens. Jerusalem, in the typical philosophical parlance, represents faith and revelation; Athens represents reason and logic. One could write an entire book on the interplay between Jerusalem and Athens (in fact, I did—check out *The Right Side of History* for a more comprehensive investigation into the topic).

To boil down that broad philosophical investigation, however, the philosophy of the Lion is based on three central principles:

1. There is a master plan, a Logos behind the universe.
2. You are made in the image of God.
3. You have true and meaningful moral duties in this world.

The First Principle of the Lion:
There Is a Master Plan

In the time of the ancients, man was seen as a mere victim of the conspiratorial gods. In *The Iliad*, human characters do their best to wage war and make love, to forge peace and protect their friends—but all their actions are thwarted or dictated secretly by this cadre of higher beings, with their own corrupt motivations.

This divine conspiracy theory is enervating (and, as we will see, it is still quite commonly held). If you have no actual way to navigate a chaotic world controlled by external forces, resignation is the most plausible response. As Achilles tells Priam, whose sons have been slaughtered at the hands of the Greeks, "So the immortals spun our lives that we, we wretched men live on to bear such torments—the gods live free of sorrows."[1]

The pagan outlook leaves us with an inevitable choice between stoic resignation, depressive acknowledgment, and impotent rage. If we are simply buffeted by the whims of the gods, there isn't all that much we can do about it. In this vision, we are all inescapably weak and powerless, searching among the ruins for our daily bread. In the words of Gloucester in *King Lear*, "As flies to wanton boys are we to the gods; They kill us for their sport."

By contrast, the First Principle—that there is a logic to the universe—lies at the heart of biblical thinking. It springs from the *rejection* of chaotic paganism. The biblical worldview says that God stands at the heart of creation: that there is a Master Planner who stands behind the world, that the world we inhabit is His creation—and that God himself is unendingly concerned with our lives and our fates. In the biblical vision, God is the source of all things—but He is good, and so is His world.

This First Principle—the understandability of the universe—cannot be proven by science. During the early nineteenth century, so the story goes, French astronomer Pierre-Simon de Laplace was having a conversation with French Emperor Napoleon, explaining to him his theory of the beginnings of the universe. "Where does God fit into all this?" Napoleon supposedly asked. "I have no need of such a hypothesis," de Laplace replied.

But de Laplace was wrong. Ironically enough, the starting point of science is the totally unprovable precept that the universe is understandable and logical. Without an understandable universe of predictable rules, searching for such rules would be a waste of time. That was Isaac Newton's point when he stated, "This most beautiful system of the sun, planets and comets, could only proceed from the counsel and dominion of an intelligent and powerful being. This Being governs all things, not as the soul of the world, but as Lord over all."[2] This does not mean that God's physical intervention is required to move the spheres, as ancient and medieval philosophers believed. It means simply that the very notion of a causal universe of discernable rules is a *faith* assumption—and that anyone who seeks answers in the universe relies on that assumption, whether explicitly or implicitly. Those who proclaim the uselessness of the Divine rely on the Divine in order to define their own purpose in life.

Every thriving civilization has a foundation in the First Principle.

It is upon that foundation that Lions build.

Lions build, because they know that there is a foundation upon which to do so.

The Second Principle of the Lion:
You Are Made in the Image of God

The Second Principle—that man has personal capability—again stems from biblical thinking. Other cultures had vested great leaders with the power of creativity and choice—epic heroes and kings were given freedom of action, but the common man was either ignored or treated as a plaything of the fates. The Bible, however, devolved authority and responsibility to each and every human being. Genesis 1:27 dictates, "God created man in His image, in the image of God He created him; male and female He created them." What does it mean to be created in the image of God? It means to be stamped with the attribute that makes God unique: the capacity to take creative action in the world. This is the message of the story of Cain and Abel, in which God tests Cain by rejecting his sacrifice and accepting Abel's. God asks Cain, "Why are you angry? And why has your face fallen? Surely, if you do right, there is uplift. But if you do not do right, sin crouches at the door. Its urge is toward you, but you can master it."

In the world of the biblical God, in short, man is *capable of choice*. His success and failures are, in the main, on his own head. God is not a conspiratorial force; God is good, and so is the universe that He created, even if it is filled with difficulty and pain. To thrive in the face of the challenges we face makes us a success; to blame others or nature or God is to fail to live up to our humanity. As Moses tells the Jews in Deuteronomy:

> See, I set before you today life and prosperity, death and destruction. For I command you today to love the Lord, your God, to walk in obedience to him, and to keep his commands,

decrees and laws. . . . Now choose life, so that you and your children may live.[3]

This principle—the capacity and responsibility of men and women—is deeply embedded in Greek thought as well. Plato stated, "[M]anaging, ruling, and deliberating, and all such things—could we justly attribute them to anything other than a soul and assert that they are peculiar to it? . . . Further, what about living? Shall we not say that it is the work of a soul?" To the biblical admonition to choose wisely, the Greeks added the importance of acting *rationally*: As Aristotle suggested, "the work of a human being is an activity of soul in accord with reason."

Lions act with deliberation and reason.

Lions understand and shoulder their power of choice.

The Third Principle of the Lion: You Have Moral Duties

The Third Principle—that we have a defined moral duty, a purpose in the world that is not our own and that we inherit—is the final piece of the philosophy of the Lion. The Lion understands that we do not create our own moral system; that our very identity represents the intersection of personal autonomy and external duties we owe to God and one another.

The Lion knows that there *are* objective moral duties in the world, proper ways of acting. Again, this is implicit in the biblical worldview: God gives us commandments because there *is* a right and there *is* a wrong. The Bible does not believe in a morally relativistic universe in which men decide what is good in their own eyes. The book of Proverbs states, "The fear of the Lord is the beginning of wisdom; fools despise wisdom and discipline. My son, heed the discipline of your father, and do not forsake the instruction of your mother."

The West relies not on free-floating reason in matters of morality, but on received tradition. Society, says eighteenth-century British philosopher and politician Edmund Burke, is indeed a contract, but it is not a contract between freewheeling atomistic individuals who come together only for some designated purpose from some phantom state of nature. Society is, instead, the result of rules and rights evolved over the course of generations—and this means we are bound to act rightly by a set of morals that precedes and will long outlast us:

> [Society and the state are] to be looked on with other reverence; because it is not a partnership in things subservient only to the gross animal existence of a temporary and perishable nature. It is a partnership in all science; a partnership in all art; a partnership in every virtue, and in all perfection. As the ends of such a partnership cannot be obtained in many generations, it becomes a partnership not only between those who are living, but between those who are living, those who are dead, and those who are to be born.

This does not mean that the rules of a society must never change, or that the Third Principle demands fundamentalist theocracy. After all, every moral principle requires interpretation. But it does mean that morality must be pegged to something beyond the malleable reason of individuals. This means *respect for moral tradition*. G. K. Chesterton explained the concept with something that came to be known as Chesterson's fence; foolish reformers see a fence in a field and, not knowing what it is, quickly demand its removal. The intelligent reformer, says Chesterston, answers,

> "If you don't see the use of it, I certainly won't let you clear it away. Go away and think. Then, we you can come back and tell me that you do see the use of it, I may allow you to destroy it."

We in the West are recipients of a moral tradition. That tradition has proved its value over the course of millennia. One need not be a God-believer to recognize this truth—or to recognize the value of that tradition. As economist Thomas Sowell writes in his masterwork, *Knowledge and Decisions*, "History is a vast storehouse of experience from generations and centuries past. So are traditions which distill the experiences of millions of other human beings over millennia of time."[4] Even myth can act as a transmitter of effective wisdom, says Sowell: "Science is no more certain to be correct than is myth. Many scientific theories have been proven wrong by scientific methods, while great enduring beliefs which have achieved the status of myths usually contain some important—if partial—truth."[5] Or as Friedrich A. Hayek writes, men use tools called "'traditions' and 'institutions'... because they are available to him as a product of cumulative growth without ever having been designed by any one mind."[6] And neither Sowell nor Hayek could properly be called a biblical believer.

In the viewpoints of both Jerusalem and Athens, acting consonant with moral duty is the obligation of a human being, and brings with it fulfillment. As King Solomon says in Ecclesiastes, "The sum of the matter, when all is said and done: Revere God and observe His commandments!" Both Plato and Aristotle believed in the natural law: that nature itself was designed toward a *telos*, an end, by an underlying logic, a *Logos*. To achieve happiness was to order oneself in coordination with the universe through the use of reason. This was Plato's answer to the challenge of Glaucon, who asked why a person ought to bother being moral: Human beings are *improperly ordered* if they act immorally.

Lions fulfill their purpose. As Aristotle put it, "What, then, prevents one from calling happy someone who is active in accord with complete virtue and who is adequately equipped with external goods, not for any chance time but in a complete life?" Virtue can only be instilled through *practice*. Some are born with fewer temptations toward sin; they are certainly lucky. But everyone has the capacity to *cultivate* virtue. This is Adam's first task in the Garden of Eden: to "serve it and to guard it."

Virtue does not grow wild. It must be cultivated.

Whether building or destroying, Lions take responsibility for their actions.

Ethics of the Fathers teaches, "In a place where there are no men, strive to be a man."

We are all called to the work. Rudyard Kipling writes in his poem "The Glory of the Garden":

> *There's not a pair of legs so thin, there's not a head so thick,*
> *There's not a hand so weak and white, nor yet a heart so sick,*
> *But it can find some needful job that's crying to be done,*
> *For the Glory of the Garden glorifieth everyone.*[7]

To sacrifice in the name of cultivating the garden, no matter your personal feelings, in spite of your own interests—this is the way of the Lion.

In August Wilson's play *Fences*, Troy—a disappointed former Negro League star relegated because of racial discrimination to life as a blue-collar garbageman—is confronted by his son, Cory. Troy and Cory constantly butt heads, particularly because Troy opposes Cory's desire to seek a football scholarship. In the most memorable scene in the play, Cory demands to know why Troy doesn't like him. Troy's answer is a perfect embodiment of the Third Principle:

> Like you? I go out of here every morning . . . bust my butt . . . putting up with them crackers every day . . . cause I like you? You about the biggest fool I ever saw. It's my job. It's my responsibility! You understand that? A man got to take care of his family. You live in my house . . . sleep you behind on my bedclothes . . . fill you belly up with my food . . . cause you my son. You my flesh and blood. Not cause I like you! Cause it's my duty to take care of you. I owe a responsibility to you. . . . Don't you try and go through life worry about if somebody like you or not. You best be making sure they doing right by you.

Of course, one could describe fulfillment of the Third Principle as love. As Golde sings in *Fiddler on the Roof* when asked by her husband, Topol, whether she loves him, "For twenty-five years I've lived with him / Fought with him, starved with him . . . If that's not love, what is?"

Duty is love, and love duty.

In Hebrew, the word for love is written אהבה. The root of the word is הב—to give. Love and duty are not merely intertwined; they are one and the same. The book of John makes the same point: "Greater love hath no man than this: that a man lay down his life for his friends."

We have no greater love than to live our lives for our friends, our family, our children, and our civilization.

The world is a place filled with those who shirk duty, who blame the world for their own failures. In that world, the Lions are those who do the opposite: They take the load upon their own shoulders. They bear the burden and reap the rewards of that task. They look in the mirror and ask, "What more can I do?"

While visiting Jerusalem, I prayed next to a twenty-one-year-old soldier in the Israel Defense Forces, or IDF.

He was a kid—closer to the age of my ten-year-old daughter than to my age—and yet he had been called to serve. While in Gaza fighting Hamas, he had been gravely wounded in an explosion in Zeitoun; he'd been airlifted to Soroka Medical Center, where both of his legs had been removed, as well as one hand. Doctors placed him in a medically induced coma, where he remained for two months.

After praying next to this young hero, I turned to leave. He tapped me on the arm—from his motorized wheelchair—and asked, "I have a question, Ben."

I nodded and gestured for him to go on.

"How else can I help?" he asked. "What's your advice for what more I can do?"

This attitude isn't unique to Israel, of course. It's the attitude of every parent who goes the extra mile, every worker who stays the extra hour, and every Western soldier who looks into the face of evil and mounts up. It is the message of Isaiah when he takes up the challenge of God:

> Then I heard the voice of my Sovereign saying, "Whom shall I send? Who will go for us?"
> And I said, "Here I am; send me."

These are the Lions.

The philosophy of the Lion is clear and direct and *good*:

There is a logic to the universe.

You are created in the image of God, which means that you have the creative power to choose—and that means you have responsibility for your choices.

The world is a place filled with moral duties—duties that spring not from your own desires and feelings, but from God, from tradition, and from reason. Fulfill those duties and you will fill your life with meaning.

All of this presupposes a *society*.

But who are the Lions who comprise this society, this civilization?

We turn to that question next.

CHAPTER TWO

THE PRIDE

JERUSALEM, ISRAEL

I write these words in Jerusalem.

The city of David.

The city of Jesus.

The city where the West was born.

This is my first visit since the October 7, 2023, massacre, since Israel's massive response in Gaza, since the opening of a multifront war by Israel's enemies—Lebanon in the north, the Houthis in Yemen in the south, the Iranian-backed Shia militias of Syria and Iraq, and Iran herself. Prior to the war, Israel was riven by deep political division: large protests every Saturday night, unhinged language about the possibility of economic collapse or even civil war.

And yet now, as we walk through the streets of Mahane Yehuda, the bustling and thriving market center of the city, the night air refreshing us, the streets are full. Israel is a late-night country—people don't go to bed until deep in the evening—and so even children run around the narrow market streets. Men and women in army uniforms, armed with M4s, stand chatting and smoking outside restaurants.

Just an hour's drive away, the brothers, fathers, and husbands of these same soldiers are serving in Gaza, moving house-to-house in the night, attempting to uncover hostages and kill terrorists.

A few nights ago, the Israel Defense Forces performed one of the most astonishing rescue operations in modern history. Four Israeli captives—Noa Argamani, Shlomi Ziv, Almog Meir Jan, and Andrey Kozlov—had been kidnapped on October 7 at the Nova Music Festival. The images of Argamani in particular became infamous: She was forced onto a motorcycle while crying and shouting, "Don't kill me!"

The four hostages were held by Gazan civilians—Hamas sympathizers paid for the privilege of holding the kidnap victims—in two separate apartments in Nuseirat, a major city in the center of the Gaza Strip. There they were starved and beaten, deprived of air and sunshine.

For months, the IDF searched for them.

Then they received information that the hostages were being held in Nuseirat. But they required confirmation. Posing as refugees from another part of the Gaza Strip, members of special forces placed themselves in Nuseirat, seeking further intelligence. They finally received confirmation of the location of the hostages. And then they launched a daring raid, freeing the hostages amid a frenzy of enemy fire.

Counterterrorism unit commando chief inspector Arnon Zamora, thirty-six, died during the rescue attempt. He left a wife and two small children. A few weeks earlier, Zamora had written a message for his fellow soldiers:

> The memory of the friends is still sharp and clear and their actions still resonate and make waves. Every day more and more

details are revealed about that cursed Saturday and what we had to deal with. That day made me even more aware of how lucky I am. I was privileged to serve by your side.... The team stands at the decisive points and I want you to know that I wouldn't ask for anyone else next to me but you. Celebrate our 76 years of independence—it is you who have made it possible and are making it possible. It is you and your families who are sacrificing for all. I want you to know how proud I am and how I love you.

Western civilization is filled with people like Arnon Zamora. People who stand when asked to defend their families and their country. Who take all the adversity life can throw at them, and keep coming. Who ask not what the world can do for them, but what they must do for the world.

These are the followers of King David, who told his son Solomon on his deathbed:

I go the way of all the earth; be you strong therefore, and show yourself a man. Keep the charge of the Lord your God, to walk in His ways, to keep His statutes, and His commandments, and His judgments, and His testimonies, as it is written in the Torah of Moses, that you may prosper in all that you do, and wherever you turn yourself.

These are the hunters.
These are the warriors.
These are the weavers.
These are the Lions.

THE HUNTERS

Survival relies on those who hunt.
    Lions hunt.
    This is a simple reality. It is not unjust, unkind, or indecent.
    As Kipling writes:

> The Jackal may follow the Tiger, but, Cub, when thy whiskers are grown,
> Remember the Wolf is a hunter—go forth and get food of thine own.[1]

    The world is a place of limited resources. This means that in order to survive—and to allow the pride to thrive—Lions must outperform, either physically or mentally. The fastest and strongest Lions historically won the race for resources: In ancient societies, the most fearsome warrior generally became the leader. No wonder the ancient kings declared themselves the chosen of the gods, and bragged of their power. The Behistun Inscription, dictated by the Persian King Darius the Great around the turn of the fifth century BC, reads both as a promise to allies and a warning to enemies:

> I am Darius, the great king, king of kings, the king of Persia, the king of countries, the son of Hystaspes, the grandson of Arsames, the Achaemenid. . . . I restored to the people, and the pasture lands, and the herds and the dwelling places, and the houses which Gaumâta, the Magian, had taken away. I settled the people in their place, the people of Persia, and Media, and

the other provinces. I restored that which had been taken away, as is was in the days of old. . . . I have ruled according to righteousness. Neither to the weak nor to the powerful did I do wrong. Whosoever helped my house, him I favored; he who was hostile, him I destroyed.

There was another model for the provider of ancient times: the gods, who could provide plenty from scarcity. The Greek god Zeus, according to myth, had to be spirited away from Cronus, the father who would eat him. He was protected by a goat, Amaltheia, who nourished him on milk. Zeus, growing powerful, snapped off one of her horns—a horn that then became a wellspring of continual nourishment, the so-called cornucopia. The cornucopia became both a Greek and Roman symbol of plenty.

But there was no true cornucopia in ancient times. Human beings could not stretch beyond the limitations of geographic reach, of primitive technology, of the expansive cost of time.

In today's world, however, the cornucopia is real.

That is, thanks to innovation and innovators.

Pure physical might—the ability to raise a roving band or to amass laborers to work the fields—is no longer the main attribute of the hunter. The hunter no longer wanders the physical savannas in search of sustenance for the pride. Today hunters are *innovators*. The ancients would have called innovation *magic*.

Innovators have stretched the very nature of our world.

Because we live amid historic plenty, we forget that the natural state of the world is *poverty*, not wealth. For nearly all of human history, *no one* was wealthy, at least not by today's standards.

In fact, the richest man in human history was poor by today's standards.

The richest man in history was likely Mansa Musa, ruler of the Mali Empire during the fourteenth century. As the master of a swath of land ranging from modern-day Niger to the western coastline of Africa, he presided over nearly half the world's known gold at the time. Mansa Musa nearly bankrupted Cairo thanks to his vast stockpile of the precious metal: He visited the city while on the way to visit Mecca and distributed so much gold that he radically inflated the currency *for a decade*. He traveled with a retinue of some 60,000 men, including the royal court and well over 10,000 slaves, all clad in gold.

Mansa Musa owned more gold than anybody who has ever lived. And in pure monetary terms, that gold is worth far more today than it was in 1337. But gold isn't *wealth*. Wealth is *better living*. By that standard, Mansa Musa—and everybody else living in 1337—was poor compared to normal citizens today.

Mansa Musa died at the age of fifty-seven, in 1337. The average citizen of a Western nation can now expect to live at least two decades longer, and in many cases, three. Mansa Musa never sat on a working toilet. Neither did anyone else of the time. Right around the time of Mansa Musa's death, the Black Death was ripping through Europe, killing one-third of the population. Mansa Musa took *two years* to travel from his empire to Mecca. Today one could make the flight in six hours. Mansa Musa would have to have waited months or years to hear replies to his correspondence. Today the poorest citizens of the world have magical devices that allow them to talk to anyone else on the planet with the press of a button.

Mansa Musa was certainly richer than anyone else of his time. But he lived in a nonwealthy world, which meant that he lived a life of relative privation—a world of horrific sights and smells, of infant mortality and illiteracy, of discomfort and disease. Yes, he owned a lot of a particular type of nonrusting yellow metal. But that doesn't make you wealthy. The only thing that makes you wealthy are the goods, products, and services available to you. Put the richest man in the world on a desert island without access to the rest of the world, and he'd be as poor as a church mouse.

So, what changed things?

Innovators.

All the materials we currently use in all our technology have existed on earth before mankind. But it took innovators to turn those materials into things worth having.

Take, for example, sand.

Sand has existed for literally all of human history. It is one of the most plentiful substances on earth: There are approximately 7.5 sextillion grains of sand on the planet. Sand was, for nearly all of human history, not only useless but annoying: It got between your toes, damaged your home, and generally made itself a nuisance.

Today, sand is one of the most important stores of value on the planet. The silicon dioxide in sand is processed in order to make silicon. Then it is processed again. And again. And again. The silicon is processed until it is 99.9999 percent pure. It is then poured to create ingots, which are then sliced into infinitesimally thin wafers. Those wafers are then polished, sent to a semiconductor fabrication plant—and become the basis for microprocessors in all of our advanced technology.

So, what changed?

Not the sand.

Innovation over time.

Every thing we take for granted is the product of human ideas building on one another in organic fashion over the course of centuries. We take for granted the fact that sludge that seeps out of the ground now powers nearly all of our economy—we know that oil is valuable now, but for centuries petroleum was used as adhesive for patching roofs.

What changed?

Innovation.

Lions *innovate*.

Innovation is a form of creative problem-solving—and lions, first and foremost, *solve problems*.

Lions do not withdraw from situations they find unpleasant, nor do they respond with volatility to problems. When faced with difficulty, their first response isn't flight—it's fight. Problems, in the view of the Lions, are merely obstacles that have not yet been surmounted. Problems are not threats to identity; they are not challenges to the very structure of the world itself. Problems are inevitabilities to the Lions. As Marcus Aurelius writes:

> Is your cucumber bitter? Throw it away. Are there briars in your path? Turn aside. That is enough. Do not go on to say, "Why were things of this sort ever brought into the world?" The student of nature will only laugh at you....[2]

Lions understand that in order to solve any problem, the first move is to think about the problem thoroughly and from nearly every angle. This means that withdrawal from problems *makes problems worse*. What's more, the Lion understands that there are rarely perfect solutions to any problem—merely a series of decisions that must be made. As Robert Pirsig, author of *Zen and the Art of Motorcycle Maintenance*, writes, "We just have to keep going until we find out what's wrong or find out why we don't know what's wrong."[3]

Because Lions seek to understand and solve problems, they work from the fundamental assumption that problems *are* solvable—if they fail, they blame themselves rather than others. Jim Collins, author of *Good to Great*, breaks down the difference between the best and the worst sales leaders. The worst, when experiencing problems, looked out the window for someone to blame; the best looked in the mirror "to apportion responsibility, never blaming bad luck when things go poorly."[4]

Lions take the lead in doing the work.

The assumption, all too often, is that those who succeed in society work the least. That is absolutely untrue. Those who build societies work diligently at whatever they do. Elon Musk famously slept on the factory floor at Tesla when production ran behind. Bill Gates began working insane hours at the ripe age of thirteen. Thomas Edison supposedly worked nearly twenty hours per day—and then, as he aged, cut back to a mere eighteen hours per day.

That doesn't mean that every Lion must work unhealthy hours. It does mean, however, that Lions *value* industriousness. That's not just true of inventors and innovators. It's true of parents, who put their entire lives into raising their children. It's true of employees who clock in and put their best into what they do. As Psalms 128 says, "When you eat of the labor of your hands, you will be happy and all will be well with you."

And finally, Lions are audacious.

Innovators are willing to go forth into the wilderness. As Abraham did in the Bible, they leave a land they know for one they have yet to be shown. America as a country was built by innovators—pioneers who crossed mountains and forded rivers to settle on land they did not know. The admonition "Go west, young man!" sounds romantic rather than insane, but for the risk-averse, it would have been closer to insanity than romance to leave the civilization of New York City and embark on a journey across thousands of miles, through hostile territory, to plant the sprigs of new beginnings elsewhere. Yet that is precisely what the pioneers did. As historian David McCullough writes, "[they] had finished their work, each in his or her own way, and no matter the adversities to be faced, propelled as they were by high, worthy purpose. They accomplished what they had set out to do not for money, not for possessions or fame, but to advance the quality and opportunities of life—to propel as best they could the American ideals."[5]

The pioneer spirit is not unique to those who forge into the physical wilderness. Pioneers can be found in all industries—the pioneers of the mind and spirit, the entrepreneurs and inventors, are lions as well. Alexis de Tocqueville noted just this attitude—what we might call the American spirit—in his *Democracy in America*:

> The people have all the wants and cravings of a growing creature.... It is not the ruin of a few individuals which may be soon repaired, but the inactivity and sloth of the community at large which would be fatal to such a people. Boldness of enterprise is the foremost cause of its rapid progress, its strength, and its greatness.[6]

That American spirit has led to global economic domination. Unchecked innovation, not altruism, is the jet fuel that powers the world. As Ayn Rand put it, "America's abundance was created not by public sacrifices to 'the common good,' but by the productive genius of free men."[7]

Innovators do not jump at every foolish chance. But they *do* and *must* take risk. Elon Musk told his biographer Walter Isaacson, "I want to keep taking risks. I don't want to savor things.... I guess I've always wanted to push my chips back on the table or play the next level of the game. I'm not good at sitting back."[8] Steve Jobs encouraged Stanford graduates to "Stay Hungry. Stay Foolish."[9]

The best hunters are those who solve problems, who put their nose to the grindstone, and who think creatively and leap into action. A worthy civilization nurtures and rewards such innovators. A worthy civilization teaches its children constant curiosity, steadfast resilience, clever adaptation, courageous trailblazing.

A worthy civilization also allows failure, because failure is the mother of success. Failure isn't a punishment. It's the reality that occurs when success isn't achieved.

The stick of failure is the catalyst toward further attempts.

Most of the time, the entrepreneur fails. According to the Bureau of Labor Statistics, approximately one in four new businesses fail within the first year. After ten years, the number is closer to two-thirds.[10] But many of these failures are launched by those who later learn from their mistakes and launch more successful companies: Most major entrepreneurs have failed repeatedly. Henry Ford famously launched two automobile companies that failed before launching Ford Motor Company, leading him to supposedly quip, "Failure is simply the opportunity to begin again, this time more intelligently."

Before my business partners and I launched *The Daily Wire*, we attempted several businesses. One was called Truth Revolt, and it was a political website associated with a midsized conservative nonprofit; I was the editor of the website, and my business partner Jeremy Boreing was the managing editor. Jeremy, being an entrepreneurial sort, began to do research into how we could maximize our traffic. He discovered that certain social media—particularly Facebook at that time—were tremendous engines for growth. His proposal was simple: If we spent money marketing our material on Facebook, we would be able to then send traffic to our website, generating advertising and subscription revenue.

This seemed to be quite a brilliant insight. So Jeremy and I were excited to present his plan to the board of that nonprofit.

Unfortunately, the board of the nonprofit was largely composed of elderly people who didn't seem to understand the internet.

Now, between the two of us, Jeremy has become known as the Stupid Whisperer, a name acquired during a long meeting with a congressperson—a meeting during which I, as a fast-talking Jew from Los Angeles, signally failed to explain a relatively simple concept to the congressperson, but Jeremy, being a slow-talking Texan, somehow explained precisely the same concept in nearly the same words, leading to a "Eureka!" moment from said elected official.

But in that meeting, Jeremy's stupid whispering wasn't working.

After nearly an hour of Jeremy explaining our business concept over and over and over, one of the board members finally turned to me and said, "Can you simplify this?"

I have to admit my irritation got the better of me.

I picked up a pen, grabbed a napkin, and wrote this:

$$\$ \to \text{FACEBOOK} \to \text{WEBSITE}$$

"We spend money on Facebook," I explained. "Facebook directs traffic to our website. That generates money, which we then reinvest. Easy."

The next week, they fired Jeremy.

The day after, I quit.

I quit because Jeremy was my business partner and good friend—and because we knew that our idea was good. We knew that we couldn't succeed in a place where there was a lid on success, and we knew that we *could* succeed if conditions were right.

Now, this is a story of failure. There are lots of things we did wrong: We probably could have presented our plan better or more cogently. We could have experimented and tried it out before making a big pitch.

But that's not the point of the story.

The point is that we then took that same plan, found investors, and built *The Daily Wire*, which became the largest online conservative media company in the world, with hundreds of employees and millions of consumers.

The harshness of failure breeds success for those who keep trying.

If we had been placed sympathetically on the government dole, paid not to work, subsidized to abandon our idea, our business never would have been born. Hundreds of employees would never have drawn a salary from us.

Now, we could have just as easily have failed again. And we would have learned from our failures. But the lesson is clear: Hunters can only improve themselves and the Pride by entering the crucible of risk and reward.

A worthy civilization raises hunters.

THE WARRIORS

The Pride cannot survive merely thanks to the innovators. That which is created must be protected. No successful civilization can be built without those willing to stand atop the gates, challenging its enemies. Those who seek to harm the Pride must be destroyed, or at least credibly threatened with destruction.

Lions, therefore, are *warriors*.

Now, all cultures have warriors—and as we'll see, Scavengers have their own brand of violence. But the West is characterized by a particular type of warrior: the citizen soldier. The citizen soldier is not a full-time soldier; he is a man dedicated to the preservation of his civilization, who picks up arms when called upon, only to return to his life as a civilian citizen when a crisis passes. And in battle, the citizen soldier defeats the scavenger on a consistent basis.

Western ways of war, as historian Victor Davis Hanson points out, have made "Europeans the most deadly soldiers in the history of civilization." Why, precisely, should that be the case? Hanson says that the "formal and often legal recognition of a person's sovereign sphere of individual action—social, political, and cultural—is a uniquely Western concept." And such individualism gives people a stake in their own futures. That freedom comes with responsibility: Each man takes his place in the phalanx of his civilization, and he fights until the war is won. This set of ideas—civic militarism, rooted in individualism and its attendant rights—determines whether warriors succeed or fail. As Hanson says:

> Abstractions like capitalism or civic militarism are hardly abstract at all when it comes to battle, but rather concrete realities

that ultimately determined whether at Lepanto twenty-year-old Turkish peasants survived or were harpooned in the thousands, whether Athenian cobblers and tanners could return home in safety after doing their butchering at Salamis or were to wash up in chunks on the shores of Attica.[11]

The language of civic militarism rings throughout Western history. It can be found in the words of Pericles, who reminded his soldiers before their 432 BC battle against the Persians, "we must resist our enemies in any and every way, and try to leave to those who come after us an Athens that is as great as ever."[12]

It can be found in the words of Abraham Lincoln, who told soldiers of the 166th Ohio Regiment in 1864, "It is not merely for today, but for all time to come that we should perpetuate for our children's children this great and free government, which we have enjoyed all our lives. I beg you to remember this, not merely for my sake, but for yours. . . . The nation is worth fighting for, to secure such an inestimable jewel."[13]

It can be most colorfully found in the words of General George S. Patton, who famously admonished his troops before the D-Day invasion:

> Americans love to fight. All real Americans love the sting and clash of battle. When you were kids, you all admired the champion marble shooter, the fastest runner, the big-league ball players and the toughest boxers. Americans love a winner and will not tolerate a loser. Americans play to win all the time. That's why Americans have never lost and will never lose a war. . . . All right, you sons of bitches. You know how I feel. I'll be proud to lead you wonderful guys in battle anytime, anywhere. That's all.[14]

This is individualist language, applied to the common cause—citizens forged into a phalanx of fighting men. And it is the language of victory—a language that lions must never stop speaking. The tradition of the West, says Hanson, is to "end hostilities quickly, decisively, and utterly."[15]

Victory in war cannot be purchased cheaply. Lions know this. That's why Israeli Prime Minister Golda Meir lamented the costs of war—not for Israelis, but for Israel's enemies—explaining in 1969, "When peace comes we will perhaps in time be able to forgive the Arabs for killing our sons, but it will be harder for us to forgive them for having forced us to kill their sons."[16]

War is hideous. And Lions know that when it is necessary, it must be fought to the end, without remorse. The main question in war is precisely how to achieve the fastest and most bloodless victory possible. All other questions are secondary.

In September 1864, General William Tecumseh Sherman penned a letter to the politicians of Atlanta after occupying the city. He wrote:

> You cannot qualify war in harsher terms than I will. War is cruelty, and you cannot refine it; and those who brought war into our Country deserve all the curses and maledictions a people can pour out. I want peace, and believe it (can) only be reached through union and war, and I will ever conduct war with a view to perfect and early success. But my dear sirs when Peace does come, you may call on me for any thing.[17]

The warrior ethos doesn't mean constant war. In fact, it is the best guarantor of peace. After examining every international conflict between 1700 and 1988, historian Geoffrey Blainey came to precisely that conclusion: "Anything which increases the optimism [of the enemy] is a cause of war. Anything which dampens that optimism is a cause of peace."[18] The credible threat of overwhelming force is an excellent damper to the optimism of the Scavenger.

Donald Trump understood this attitude thoroughly as president. Despite all of the complaints about him, the first Trump administration's foreign policy resulted in the most peaceful world of any modern president. That was not because of the complexity and nuance of his foreign policy positions. It's because Trump made clear to the world that if he was pushed too far, the consequences would be disastrous for America's enemies.

During a fundraiser at the Trump National Doral club in Miami, Trump explained it to me this way.

"Do you know why Vladimir Putin never invaded Ukraine while I was president?" he said. "It's because I said, 'Vladimir, if you go into Ukraine, I will bomb the s*** out of you.'"

"And Vladimir said, 'Mr. President, no, you won't.'"

"And," said Trump, completing the story, "I said, 'Well, Vladimir, I *might*.' And here's the thing: If our enemies think there's a five percent chance that they will end up at war with the most powerful military in the history of the planet, they tend not to risk it."

THE WEAVERS

A Pride of Lions requires more than entrepreneurial innovation and aggressive defense. It requires *social fabric*. No society composed entirely of hunters and warriors could survive intact—every society requires those who hold together families, who build communities, who care for the sick and the elderly. Every society requires *weavers*.

Weavers are those who build the institutions of a society, who knit together disparate elements into a broader whole. At the end of George Eliot's *Middlemarch*, the heroine of the novel, Dorothea, discovers that she need not strive for personal greatness in order to achieve happiness, goodness, and a beneficent effect on the world. As Eliot concludes:

> the growing good of the world is partly dependent on unhistoric acts; and that things are not so ill with you and me as they might have been, is half owing to the number who lived faithfully a hidden life, and rest in unvisited tombs.[19]

These are the weavers—those who go largely unnoticed, who do the daily work of childcare and teaching, of PTA meetings and social clubs, of local government and charity work. These are the Lions who pass on, through their daily activity, the wisdom of the institutions by which they are shaped and that they spend their lives maintaining. They sweep the floors and pay the taxes and give the charity and visit the sick. They rarely receive full-page obituaries in the major newspapers. But at their funerals, members of their Pride testify to their self-sacrifice, their generosity, their goodness.

All of us know weavers—those who sew together the sinews of our society. They appear throughout our lives at different times, almost providentially, spurring us forward and binding us together.

My wife is such a person.

She is brilliant in her own right—a family physician who earned her medical degree through hard work at UCLA Medical School. She is a pillar of our community; she involves herself daily in the local school, the synagogue, and a multiplicity of charities. She ensures that our household—indeed, our entire lives—run; she comforts our children when they are upset and holds them to account when they misbehave; she brings them to their medical appointments and helps them with their homework and plays with them and tells them bedtime stories. She takes care of her parents and goes out of her way for her friends.

And then, after the kids go to bed, she listens to me grouse about my day and the travails of the world.

I knew my wife was a weaver from the time I met her. It was built into her character. The winds of life batter everyone, but the weavers ensure that the sails never tear away, and that the ship of family and community can sail on.

Certain qualities characterize the weavers.

Weavers are *prudent*. They respect wisdom and apply it to the real world. They are often the people whom others go to for advice. Because their focus is constantly on maintaining and fixing institutions—the institutions that serve as the foundation for both hunters and warriors—they inherently embody a certain prudence. They are prudent because they know that change is difficult, and radical change tears the social fabric, no matter how positive the intentions. This is why religious leaders often find themselves in the role of weaver: They are representatives of ancient wisdom, defenders of a centuries-old legacy. There is a reason Catholics consider prudence the first of the cardinal virtues; as St. Thomas Aquinas writes in *Summa Theologica*, "prudence is right reason applied to action," the application of eternal principles to matters at hand.[20] As Jesus states in the book of Matthew, "[E]veryone who hears these words of mine and puts them into practice is like a wise man who built his house on the rock. The rain came down, the streams rose, and the winds blew and beat against that house; yet it did not fall, because it had its foundation on the rock."[21]

Weavers protect the rock.

To the weavers, new threads may be added to the tapestry of community, but such an art must be applied with tremendous care. As philosopher Russell Kirk writes:

> [T]he body social is a kind of spiritual corporation, comparable to the church; it may even be called a community of souls. Human society is no machine, to be treated mechanically. The continuity, the life-blood, of a society must not be interrupted. Burke's reminder of the necessity for prudent change is in the mind of the conservative. But necessary change, conservatives argue, ought to be gradual and discriminatory, never unfixing old interests at once.[22]

Weavers are also *merciful*.

If prudence demands the application of justice, mercy demands that justice be balanced with forgiveness. God promises Adam that if he eats of the Tree of Knowledge, he will surely die—yet God doesn't slay Adam after Adam sins. Instead, God applies mercy: He clothes Adam, shielding him from his own shame and nakedness.

Society would cease to exist were justice its only rule. Forgiveness and empathy are the only way any societal institution can exist. There is *strength* in forgiveness and in empathy.

Only Lions can forgive.

In the Jewish Yom Kippur prayers, the so-called Thirteen Attributes of God are repeated by the congregation. Those Thirteen Attributes can be found in Exodus 34, when God forgives the Jews for the sin of the Golden Calf. God passes before Moses, and describes Himself:

The Lord, the Lord, the compassionate and gracious God, slow to anger, abounding in love and faithfulness, maintaining love to thousands, and forgiving wickedness, rebellion and sin.[23]

According to the Talmud, repentance was created "before the world was created."[24] Without repentance—without God's recognition that man would have to be forgiven—man could not have survived God's justice. Mercy is a divine virtue. In the words of Portia in Shakespeare's *The Merchant of Venice*, rebutting Shylock's plea for strict, by-the-letter justice:

The quality of mercy is not strained;
It droppeth as the gentle rain from heaven
Upon the place beneath. It is twice blest;
It blesseth him that gives and him that takes:
'Tis mightiest in the mightiest; it becomes
The thronèd monarch better than his crown:
His sceptre shows the force of temporal power,
The attribute to awe and majesty,
Wherein doth sit the dread and fear of kings;
But mercy is above this sceptred sway;
It is enthronèd in the hearts of kings,
It is an attribute to God himself;
And earthly power doth then show likest God's
When mercy seasons justice.[25]

It is no coincidence that throughout Western literature, the qualities of prudence and empathy have been associated with women. Prudence was frequently depicted in the Renaissance period as Prudentia, a woman holding a mirror (a gateway to introspection and knowledge) and a snake (a reference to the book of Matthew's admonition to be "wise as serpents"). The term for mercy in Hebrew—*rachamim*—is the plural form of the noun *rachum*, which literally means "womb." God's love for us, as evidenced by His mercy, is even greater than that of a mother for her child, as it states in Isaiah: "Can a woman forget her baby, or disown the child of her womb? Though she might forget, I never could forget you."[26] In Proverbs, the woman of valor is praised beyond all measure:

> *Her mouth is full of wisdom,*
> *Her tongue with kindly teaching.*
> *She oversees the activities of her household*
> *And never eats the bread of idleness. . . .*
> *Grace is deceptive,*
> *Beauty is illusory;*
> *It is for her fear of the Lord*
> *That a woman is to be praised.*[27]

The supposedly stereotypical association between prudence, mercy, and femininity is grounded in biological reality. By available data, women tend to feel and show more empathy than men; they are also, on average, more risk-averse and cautious.

But this does not mean that weavers do not take risks. To invest one's life in building the institutions of society requires risk-taking. Weavers simply take a different kind of risk, a quieter one. In many ways, the risks they take are the greatest of all.

For instance, at every level, from the biological to the psychological, marriage is a risk.

As a genetic strategy, for example, sexual reproduction is inherently risky: It means exchanging one half of one's genetics for the genetics of a stranger. Yet that risk carries with it tremendous benefit: Diversification of genetics leads to a more robust, dynamic, and durable gene pool. In fact, according to the so-called Red Queen hypothesis, sexual reproduction itself evolved in order to avoid the risks of parasitism: If parasites can replicate more easily than hosts, and are evolved to take advantage of the weaknesses of their hosts, hosts are at an inherent disadvantage. One possible evolutionary strategy, then, would be to diversify the hosts' genetic pool by abandoning asexual reproduction—reproductive strategies like cloning, which simply maintains the genetics of the original host—in favor of sexual reproduction, which changes the host's genetic offspring and thus avoids parasites. This is a risk—but it is a calculated one.

The same is true of marriage as a biological risk. A man risks giving up his ability to reproduce with a wide variety of females in favor of reproduction with one specific female, who can provide only a limited number of offspring; a woman risks her genetic offspring on one male. This risk is the basic building block of society, though—without it men remain promiscuous and irresponsible, children fatherless, and women unprotected.

Marriage is, most of all, a psychological risk. It is a leap into the darkness—for even if we love someone, the someone we love will change and grow with time. The nature of marriage is a commitment to something beyond the person we find in the moment, to an eternal bond that we wager will grow stronger and more meaningful over the course of decades. As Shakespeare puts it:

Let me not to the marriage of true minds
Admit impediments; love is not love

Which alters when it alteration finds,
Or bends with the remover to remove.[28]

Commitment to marriage is a commitment to an unknown future.

That commitment is what makes marriage a miracle and a blessing. Who in their right mind would sign up for a decades-long commitment to another person, knowing that human beings change over time? Only a fool. Only a person of faith. Only a person who understands that love grows and deepens *because of commitment itself*. As it turns out, the great risk of our lives—choosing one person and settling down with them—gives us back our greatest adventure, our greatest fulfillment, and our greatest calling.

And it results in an even *greater* task: bearing and raising children.

Children are a mystery from the day they are born until they develop as adults. What will our children be tomorrow? Ten years from now? Initiating that journey is an act of faith—and it is the greatest risk of all, given that we invest everything we have into these beings over whom, in the end, we have little control. My wife and I have four children. Nothing about their behavior is guaranteed, even from day to day. Who will they be a decade from now? Two? We have no idea. Yet we pour ourselves into our children—our love, our determination, our values—hoping that they will be the kind of people who better mankind.

Without taking such risks, mankind would fail, by definition.

Being a weaver doesn't make a person weak. It makes a person strong—fully created in the image of God, with the power to build entire civilizations. Weavers hold families, communities, and societies together. In the words of the book of Ezekiel, describing the Kingdom of David, "What a lioness was your mother among the lions! Crouching among the great beasts, she reared her cubs."[29]

Two years ago, my wife and I had our fourth child.

He was, as all children are, a squalling, ravenously hungry little creature. Children at birth aren't truly cute yet; as any visitor to a new mother will tell you, babies fresh from the womb are too vulnerable and scrawny to be adorable. They're red, they're tiny, and they spend most of the day either sleeping, nursing, or pooping.

Children are not inherently good either.

That assertion of inherent goodness, propagated mainly by those who have never met a child, is a total lie. Children lie; they are selfish; they cheat and they steal. They have few concerns other than their wants and needs.

Children must be *civilized*.

They must become Lions.

In the Jewish community, that civilizing process begins, for boys, at the age of eight days.

The Bible commands Jews to circumcise their children. The so-called *brit milah*—literally, covenant of circumcision—springs from God's command to Abraham in Genesis:

> As for me, this is My covenant with you: You shall be the father of a multitude of nations.... As for you, you and your offspring to come throughout the ages shall keep My covenant. Such shall be the covenant between Me and you and your offspring to follow which you shall keep: every male among you shall be circumcised.[30]

Circumcision isn't exactly an emotionally easy ceremony. It involves a surgical procedure in front of a large group of people on the most sensitive organ of the male body. The obvious question, of course, is *why*. And the simple answer is this: Circumcision represents entry into Abraham's covenant—a covenant of commitment to a certain set of values.

Into duty.

Upon the circumcision, the father says a blessing, invoking Abraham's covenant with God. The entire congregation then responds: "Just as he has entered into the Covenant, so may he enter into Torah, into marriage, and into good deeds."

This is an extraordinary ceremony.

It's extraordinary because it recognizes a fundamental truth: From the time we are born, we are born into a thick network of mutual obligation. We are born into roles that predate us and will outlast us. It is our job to grow into those roles: to become members of our family, of our community.

It is our job to become hunters and warriors and weavers.

To become members of the pride.

Every Lion requires a Pride. Not just in celebration, but in hardship too.

In our Jewish community in South Florida, there was a family—a family struck by tragedy. The family had a wonderful eight-year-old girl who died of brain cancer. The entire community provided physical and emotional aid and support to the family during her decline. A close friend of the family—a particularly brilliant and caring doctor—guided her medical care and went so far as to sleep in her hospital room to give her parents a break. After her death, the entire community mourned with the family: hundreds of people, coming to comfort the bereaved, night after night.

In Genesis, upon creating man, God immediately states, "it is not good for the man to be alone; I will make a fitting counterpart for him."[31] Thus God creates woman—but woman is not given her name until she has children, whereupon she becomes Eve, the mother of all living. And the society of God doesn't stop there. From family, God scales up to tribe, and from tribe to nation. In fact, the story of the Old Testament can be seen as God teaching man how to erect a society from the building blocks of families. As Burke stated, "To be attached to the subdivision, to love the little platoon we belong to in society, is the first principle (the germ as it were) of public affections. It is the first link in the series by which we proceed towards a love to our country, and to mankind."[32]

Family. Community. Nation.

Pride.

We must all be Lions.

Our Pride demands it.

But how can a civilization of Lions grow and thrive?

How can a civilization of Lions—a civilization filled with individuals who are strong, ambitious, and proud—keep from tearing itself apart?

dard by which all right-of-center media is barred from the advertising market. Advertisers and agencies that are so-called GARM "members" represent fully 90 percent of all advertising spending in the United States, and include major corporations like GroupM, NBC Universal, Procter & Gamble, Shell, Unilever, Bayer, Adidas, and Mastercard. If you're not receiving advertising dollars from GARM members, and advertising represents a significant portion of your earnings, you're probably out of business.

The House Judiciary Committee room can be an intimidating place. Before you, in a rising semicircle, sit the members of the committee—which means, physically, they're above you. You are the subject; they are the inquisitors. You sit behind a wooden table, a microphone stemming up to greet you. Behind the members are portraits of the past chairs of the committee. In front are the elected representatives of the American public.

They are, all in all, normal people—people attempting to do their best with the resources at their disposal. Some are honest public servants who have decided to give up their private lives for something they believe is more important. Others are grandstanders looking for a cable news gig.

As a witness, you have to be ready for all of it.

Today, I'm treated to the full panoply.

Many of the members ask intelligent questions about the balance between First Amendment values and censorship by large corporations, about the appropriate balance between private and public. Some are only there to make a quick headline by jabbering about the political hot topic of the day.

On this day, my bête noire turns out to be Representative Eric Swalwell (D-CA), a former short-lived presidential candidate and fre-

CHAPTER THREE

THE RULES OF THE PRIDE

WASHINGTON, DC

Everyone hates Congress.

Congress is widely despised, and for good reason: It is an enormous meetinghouse for lawyers, businessmen, career politicians, and derelicts. These categories are not mutually exclusive. A day in Congress will frustrate you, annoy you, and make you wonder—with more than a hint of anger—just how in the world the United States continues to function. Congress churns out bills thousands of pages long that nobody reads; it spends trillions of dollars for which nobody pays, at least not for the moment; it regulates, in picayune fashion, elements of American life well outside its constitutional purview.

I'm here to testify before the House Judiciary Committee, and specifically about a censorship cartel called the Global Alliance for Responsible Media (GARM). That cartel—an organization of advertising agencies that have banded together to create a set of rules about content "appropriate" for advertisers—has essentially established a stan-

quent cable news guest. Swalwell knows his role—he's here to make some viral clips. And he takes that role seriously.

We grin at each other as he takes his seat. It's time to play.

Swalwell shows up with a large posterboard quoting me about social policy—a topic that has nothing to do with the hearing. He then proceeds to grill me about my personal religious beliefs. For some reason, he seems to think that if he reads me my own words, I'll be embarrassed. Clearly, this is an attack line that is bound to fail. I respond, "Yes, I agree with me."

"Reader," Mark Twain once wrote, "suppose you were an idiot. And suppose you were a member of Congress. But I repeat myself."

A century and a half later, little has changed.

But here's the thing: While all of this is messy and imperfect and often silly, that messy, imperfect, silly system allows for the most durable and powerful republic in the history of the world. It allows citizens like me to face down representatives of a massive central government responsible for the protection of 340 million citizens. It allows the common man the ability to have a say in how his nation is governed.

Later, I will learn that the hearing itself ended up generating real change: Elon Musk, who watched the hearing, threatens to sue GARM.

And GARM actually *disbands*.

The censorship cartel is broken, at least for now; advertisers vow to look at the vast panoply of political offerings for possible advertisement. First Amendment values have been strengthened—all because we live in a system that takes account of the rights of its citizens.

I don't know any of that yet, of course.

I walk through the Capitol Rotunda on my way out.

The dome itself was built between 1856 and 1863—the time of the greatest upheaval in American history, when Americans were killing each other by the hundreds of thousands. Yet it still stands as a monument to the unity of the country. The interior of the dome bears an enormous fresco, covering nearly five thousand square feet. Titled *The Apotheosis of Washington*, it features George Washington rising toward heaven, surrounded by Liberty and Victory, as well as thirteen figures representing the original colonies. Surrounding the central figures are six other groups of figures, representing war, science, marine, commerce, mechanics, and agriculture.[1]

It puts me in mind of the Sistine Chapel—this is America's own version of creation, blessed by the Almighty. And that makes sense, given that the artist, Constantino Brumidi, originally worked in the Vatican before immigrating to the United States. But where the Sistine Chapel is all about the meeting of God and mankind, *The Apotheosis of Washington* is about the possible achievements of mankind under a system of liberty. As Brumidi said, "My one ambition and my daily prayer is that I may live long enough to make beautiful the Capitol of the one country on earth in which there is liberty."

He didn't fulfill his dream—he died before the completion of all his work in the Senate, which extended to the Rotunda frieze—and he was eventually buried in an obscure grave and forgotten. Only nearly a century later was his sacrifice uncovered and publicized.[2]

So, how do we square all of this? How do we explain the fact that a system of gridlock and rivalry, of ambition counteracting ambition, has fostered the greatest republic in the history of the world?

The answer is deceptively simple.

America is not a land of kings, nor is it a land of peasants. It is a land of Lions, because our system is *built to protect and reward Lions*. Our system is designed to prevent the Lions from being caged or being wounded; it is designed to ensure that Lions cannot tyrannize one another. And it is designed to keep those Lions aggressive and enterprising.

In short, the American system fosters the American spirit. Tocqueville described that spirit this way:

> For an American, one's entire life is spent as a game of chance, a time of revolution, a day of battle. These same causes operating at the same time on all individuals in the end impress an irresistible impulse on the national character. The American taken randomly will therefore be a man ardent in his desires, enterprising, adventurous—above all, an innovator.[3]

America provides us the freedom to succeed.

In doing so, America—and the world—reaps the benefits.

That is because America, in principle, is a true *meritocracy*.

America recognizes that while God made us all equal in our spiritual value, He certainly did not make us all the same. Such a contention would be a crime against good sense. As John Adams wrote, "It will be readily admitted, there are great inequalities of merit, or talents, virtues, services, and what is of more moment, very often of reputation."[4] Even Thomas Jefferson, author of the phrase "all men are created equal," acknowledged the reality of a "natural aristoi."[5] Adams and Jefferson were archrivals on any number of philosophical and political topics, but both understood that it would be foolish to contend that every man has the same inherent qualities as every other man.

Every individual is different. Some of us are taller, some shorter; some of us are more intelligent, some less; some more determined, some lazier. No two individuals are equal in virtually any way.

The same is true of groups. Group *averages* may or may not be equivalent in some individual measure or another, but virtually no two groups are identical. That isn't a question of genetics. That is a question of statistics. Draw a line down the middle of any room, anywhere in the world, and the two resulting groups will differ in a wide variety of respects.

But here is where we are the same: in our ability—indeed, our *obligation*—to strive.

Some will win. Some will lose.

Most of us will do a lot of both.

That is a reality.

And it is *good*.

This isn't unfair. It is, in fact, the *fairest* system available.

In a fair and good system, the system incentivizes and rewards the *meritorious*. It rewards the Lions. The Lion is strongest, best, seeks the highest good. The functional society rewards the Lion because the lion creates, builds, and maintains the society. The Lion creates positive externalities. Everyone benefits from a system that rewards the Lions. Society *must* reward the Lion, or else the Lions will die.

And then so will everyone and everything else.

A society that rewards Lions is called a *meritocracy*.

Now, in order to justify a meritocracy, one must define merit. And in order to define merit, one must define the good. The philosophy of Lions has no problem in defining merit, because the philosophy of Lions has no problem in defining the good, as we have seen: The good is to be found in fulfilling the duties of the moral system we have all inherited. Good hunters innovate and produce. Good warriors defend and protect. Good weavers build and sustain. Merit requires innovating, protecting, and building in accordance with our God-given abilities. Any system that incentivizes such merit ought to be promoted; any system that inhibits merit ought to be obliterated.

The meritocracy works.

No other system does.

Any alternative to meritocracy *definitionally* demotes merit as the standard for human achievement. Prizing any other factor over merit simply means setting up an artificial standard of pseudo-justice that lowers positive societal benefits in order to reward a choice few. Whether it is cronyism, tribalism, or aristocracy, any attempt to thwart meritocracy means rewarding Scavengers—those who leech off the true productivity of the Lions.

To determine who is a success and who is a failure requires that we allow people to succeed and to fail on their own merits. Meritocracies celebrate those who dare and dare greatly. Meritocracies celebrate *liberty* and *achievement*.

And meritocracies require rules.

It turns out that the meritorious cannot rise to the top—the meritorious cannot be fully rewarded, nor can they bestow those rewards upon others—without a framework of basic rules, embedded in workable institutions.

Those rules are simple in theory, but difficult to achieve in practice.

Free minds.

Free markets.

Public virtue.

Rule of law.

These are the rules of the Pride.

RULE #1: THE PRIDE PROTECTS FREE MINDS

The Pride—the society of Lions—cannot remain united long if it ceases to protect that which makes Lions *Lions*: the innate capacity to choose. This does not mean that choice is without consequence, or that all choices ought to be treated as morally equivalent—libertinism unwinds society, as we will soon explore. But without freedom of thought, Lions cease to be Lions and are instead reduced to the level of Scavengers, relying on the creation of others for their daily bread. What's more, the Lion robbed of his initiative loses his will and his purpose. As philosopher Isaiah Berlin beautifully expresses:

> For him man differs from animals primarily neither as the possessor of reason, nor as an inventor of tools and methods, but as a being capable of choice, one who is most himself in choosing and not being chosen for.[6]

The argument against liberty typically takes this form: If we know what is true and right, then why ought people be given the leeway to think differently? But as the West has recognized, to its infinite benefit, even a society of true virtue requires choice. In the words of Thomas Aquinas, "to believe depends on the will."[7] This notion—freedom of religion—has been a bedrock of Americanism since its inception, and is well articulated by Thomas Jefferson's 1786 Virginia Statute for Religious Freedom:

> Almighty God hath created the mind free; that all attempts to influence it by temporal punishment or burthens, or by civil

incapacitations, tend only to beget habits of hypocrisy and meanness, and are a departure from the plan of the Holy author of our religion, who being Lord both of body and mind, yet chose not to propagate it by coercions on either, as was his Almighty power to do....[8]

A society of hunters requires free minds.

After all, innovation is thinking differently; innovation adds information to a system that lacked that information before. How else could innovation occur without free minds? As Hayek observes, "If we are to advance, we must leave room for a continuous revision of our present conceptions and ideals which will be necessitated by further experience."[9] No one has a monopoly on knowledge or the ability to predict the next course in innovation—which is why we must outsource innovation and knowledge to all of humanity. That is what freedom of the mind represents.

Freedom of mind isn't merely a requirement for hunters—it is a requirement for warriors as well. One of the most distinctive aspects of the Western way of war is its reliance on devolution of authority. Contrary to popular opinion, the most successful warrior cultures are *not* run in top-down fashion—in fact, centralization of command authority typically results in stagnation and failure. Germany's blitzkrieg strategy at the inception of World War II, for example, wasn't successful because of superior machinery, many historians argue, but because command decisions were made in the field by those best positioned to achieve the strategic ends; as Hitler began to centralize command, the war went far worse for the Germans.[10] The same holds true in every military: The more initiative those who fight our wars are given, the better the results. As retired Navy SEAL commander Jocko Willink writes:

Decentralized Command was a necessity. In such situations, the leaders did not call me and ask me what they should do. Instead, they told me what they were going to do.... I trusted them to lead.[11]

The same holds true of military innovation. The Israel Defense Forces—perhaps the best example on earth of an army forced to do more with less, in the least hospitable region on the planet—must constantly innovate. And that can only happen with a radically flattened hierarchical structure and a shockingly open-door policy with regard to new ideas. As military analyst Edwin Luttwak points out, "What that means in practice is that no formal qualifications or position of authority are required to obtain a hearing for a new idea and even development funds if warranted...."[12]

Weavers, too, require freedom of thought.

No parent can raise his or her children without serious autonomy. As anyone with children knows, raising children is far more of an art than a science; children are unique, and require individualized solutions, which is why one-size-fits-all government institutionalization disserves them so radically. The same holds true in building communities. There is a reason that the Constitution of the United States guards freedom of association: We are collective beings, not merely individuals, and that means that we must have the ability to band together to build churches, synagogues, communities. Social fabric relies on freedom of mind: If we cannot speak freely with one another, no true friendship can ever be formed. The destruction of social fabric—the intermediate institutions that serve as a bulwark between the individual and government—remains a hallmark of tyrannical governments today, and relies upon evisceration of freedom of association.

RULE #2: THE PRIDE PROTECTS FREE MARKETS

Merit cannot be rewarded unless we protect the autonomy of the individual.

If his merit can be thwarted, his gains seized, his innovation punished, merit dies.

So, how do we protect autonomy?

We must have what Nobel Prize–winning economists Daron Acemoglu and James A. Robinson called *inclusive economic institutions*:

> Inclusive economic institutions ... are those that allow and encourage participation by the great mass of people in economic activities that make best use of their talents and skills and that enable individuals to make the choices they wish.[13]

Such inclusive economic institutions require a system of private property, predicable and equally applied law, provision of basic public services, and freedom of entrepreneurship.

Without these inclusive economic institutions, the meritorious cannot succeed.

With them, the meritorious rarely fail.

The meritorious require freedom to test, to rise, to fall, to get up again. They require a system that protects their investment of time and effort and capital, that guarantees that they will not awake each morning afraid of a knock at the door telling them that what they have built is no longer theirs. It is no surprise that nationalization of industries generally results in a massive drop-off in productivity:

Who would invest in a company that could simply expropriate property at any time?

In short, the Pride requires *free markets*. There are two cases in their favor.

First, the *moral case*: Free markets fulfill the creative needs of mankind and make men better in the process.

Second, the *efficiency case*: Free markets create wealth by incentivizing innovation.

Free markets create and incentivize Lions.

The Moral Case for Free Markets

You own the product of your hands.

As we have explored, one of the fundamental principles of the philosophy of lions is that *man is made in the image of God, a creative, choosing being with autonomy and power.* We thus have a right to our own labor. The philosopher John Locke, one of the great influences on the American founding, explained this right to property:

> [E]very Man has a Property in his own Person. This no Body has any Right to but himself. The Labour of his Body, and the Work of his Hands, we may say, are properly his. Whatsoever then he removes out of the State that Nature hath provided, and left it in, he hath mixed his Labour with, and joined to it something that is his own, and thereby makes it his Property.[14]

Private property goes to the essence of what it means to be a human being. Without it, creative power is denied its source. Property is embedded in nature. As historian Richard Pipes notes, "anthropologists have concluded that there never was a society so primitive as not to acknowledge some forms of ownership."[15] Every child understands this reality. By the age of two, children understand the difference between their property and the property of others; as researchers Nicholaus Noles of Michigan State University and Susan Gelman of the University of Michigan write, "[P]reschoolers demonstrate an understanding of the nuanced contrast between ownership and possession. They defend possession of an object more aggressively if they own it and strenuously object when their property rights, as well as the property rights of others, are violated."[16] Every parent knows this too: Give one of your kids an allowance for doing chores, then tell her to hand over half of her allowance to her younger brother, who has been sitting aside and casually watching television. You're likely to end up with a major and rather justifiable tantrum on your hands.

Private property is just a reality of the world: Virtually all animals, human beings most of all, innately understand and believe in ownership. Human beings then develop rules and rituals surrounding the ownership and dispensation of private property, regularizing and cultivating a set of neutral principles that enable us to live with one another.

From private property springs the system of the free market. Free markets are rooted in the simple recognition that if I own my property, I ought to be able to trade it, dispense with it, or invest it as I see fit, so long as those decisions do not infringe upon the equal rights of others.

Free markets are justice.

Free markets are just, because justice is the proposition, as Aristotle suggested, that equals should be treated equally and unequals unequally.

As we've discussed, individuals are equal in their rights but not in their qualities. I have the same rights that you do, but that does not mean that we each have precisely the same earning capacity. LeBron James and I have the same rights, but he is a far better basketball player than I am; meanwhile, I'd venture to say that I've probably read a few more books cover to cover than he has.

That isn't unjust—unless by unjust, we simply mean that we wish that God had made us all identical in every way at the outset of life. And if that's our complaint, we ought to grow up.

Anger at God for not making the world the way you would want it isn't justice. It's arrogance, stupidity, and childishness. As Thomas Sowell observes, justice is a *process*, not an outcome. We are not God, that we can "simply say, 'Let there be equality!' or 'Let there be justice!' We must begin with the universe that we were born into and weigh the costs of making any specific change in it to achieve a specific end."[17]

Inequality is not inequity; disparity is not injustice.

What *would* be unjust would be to shackle LeBron James to a tractor so that we could play basketball more equally, or to force me never to read a book so that he and I could converse on political theory on an even playing field.

In Kurt Vonnegut's dystopian short story "Harrison Bergeron," society has done just that: handicapped the outstanding in order to achieve equality. As Vonnegut writes, "[E]verybody was finally equal. They weren't only equal before God and the law. They were equal every which way. Nobody was smarter than anybody else. Nobody was better looking than anybody else. Nobody was stronger or quicker than anybody else." All that is required is that the intelligent be saddled with a mental-handicap radio sounding short bursts of sharp noise in order to keep them from taking unfair advantage of their brains; for ballerinas to be burdened with sashweights and bags of birdshot, their faces masked, so their beauty cannot be an advantage; for the physically strong to be hung with hundreds of pounds of scrap metal, so as to equalize their particular advantage.[18]

This isn't justice, of course. It is the essence of oppression.

True justice means that we each ought to have the same right to the advantage of our natural abilities.

We call that set of rights the free market.

And it sets us free. It lets us soar.

It also makes human beings better *as human beings*, not worse.

Contrary to the foolish and postulant attitude of Marxists and their ideological descendants, private property does not make us selfish; private property sets boundaries to our selfishness, since we cannot own that to which we have no right, and must respect the private property of others. Free markets do not make us dishonest; they make us far *more* honest, since a failure to recognize the difference between mine and yours inevitably leads human beings to the convenient lie that *everything is mine*. There is a reason that the cretinous anarchists of Occupy Wall Street—opponents of capitalism in the main—left a gargantuan mess behind them, while the members of the much-maligned pro-markets Tea Party generally cleaned up their trash. If you had to choose, based merely on protest attendance, whom to entrust with babysitting your child, the answer wouldn't be particularly difficult.

Free markets reward honesty, punctuality, and decency. The most successful businesspeople cannot afford to cheat their customers, lest they lose their business. As Adam Smith stated in his *Lectures on Jurisprudence*, "Whenever commerce is introduced into any country probity and punctuality always accompany it. These virtues in a rude and barbarous country are almost unknown."[19]

Free markets promote justice, hard work, innovation, and honesty. Free markets are not planned from above; they emerge from the various clamoring interests of an endlessly diverse human species, enabled with their rights to private property and rule of law. They are evolutionary. And because they are spontaneously ordered—because they themselves are the product of liberty—they produce liberty.

As Nobel Prize–winning economist and philosopher Friedrich Hayek wrote, the death of private property represents the lifeblood of tyranny; to destroy private property would allow the possibility of unending coercion, destroying the sphere of liberty, productivity, and creativity:

> [I]t has long been recognized that "a people averse to the institution of private property is without the first element of freedom" and that "nobody is at liberty to attack several property and to say at the same time that he values civilization. The history of the two cannot be disentangled."[20]

Free markets don't just allow for the free exchange of products, goods, and services. They prize diversity in the richest possible sense: They take account of every individual's needs, wants, and desires. They allow for a diversity of opinion to emerge on the value of products, goods, and services in comparison with other priorities; that diversity extends down to the level of the individual. That aggregated knowledge is called the *pricing system*.

Prices in free markets are one of the bugaboos of tyrants. They believe that free markets are unjust because they result in prices they do not personally approve. Typically, such arguments take the following form: "Why should LeBron James make more money than a second-grade teacher?" On its face, the argument seems plausible, at least emotionally: We all share the gut belief that second-grade teachers are more societally important than star basketball players.

But this critique of private property is both a lie and a category error.

First off, it is a lie, because it suggests that teachers are underpaid by some standard—that they have been evaluated for merit by the markets and found wanting. That is eminently untrue. The market for teachers has been severely restricted by regulatory influence and union cronyism; in a true free market, the best teachers would be paid many times what the worst are paid. Only the corruption of the oligarchic teachers unions and their well-funded elected officials prevents a truer market that might reward the best and most innovative teachers in line with their actual economic value.

But even under such conditions, comparing an individual teacher to LeBron James is a category error: Teachers represent an entire *market class*, while James represents his own market class—NBA players. Teachers in the United States, according to the National Education Association, earn an average salary of $71,699 annually;[21] according to the Pew Research Center, some 3.8 million public school teachers work in the classroom.[22] Meanwhile, there are generally around 550 NBA players who are on a team during an average NBA season, earning an average salary of $12 million. If we compare apples to apples, then—not one second-grade teacher in Peoria, Illinois, versus LeBron James, but total teacher expenditure versus total NBA expenditure—we find that Americans spend more than $270 billion on teachers per year, while spending just $170 million per year on NBA players. In other words, we pay our teachers nearly 1,600 times more than we pay our NBA players in the aggregate.

Herein lies the point: As investor par excellence Benjamin Graham famously stated, "[I]n the short run, the market is a voting machine, but in the long run, it is a weighing machine." Markets always act on imperfect information at any given moment, but in the long run they do an unparalleled job of evaluating collective interests and passing that information on to those who make decisions about production. This feedback loop is the single greatest way of ensuring that everyone's voice is heard.

And it is why free markets work where tyrants fail.

Marx heavily relied on the labor theory of value. He posited that if you could calculate the value of anything *objectively*, then anything beyond that value had to be a *surplus*—an unnecessary bit of profiteering added by the person selling a good, product, or service. So, if the labor value of a potato was, say, $2—the labor put into growing the potato, harvesting it, and selling it to the grocer—and the grocer sold it for $3 to an end customer, the grocer was adding on an unfair surcharge of $1, thus increasing the price falsely so as to extract *profit*. Marx said the world could be made fairer and better by preventing the grocer from extracting profit, thus lowering prices and making potatoes more affordable. The grocer was actually *exploiting* his customers when he "earned" a profit.

The answer, said Marx, was to set prices from the top down. Simply set the price of potatoes at $2, remove the grocer's evil profit, and make everything more plentiful and cheaper.

This, as it turns out, is idiocy. The price of potatoes isn't set. There is nothing about a potato that makes it $2. Why? Because the preferences of human beings are fluid. The price of a good or service is only *what we think it is*. And that price can change over time as we decide, individually, what we prioritize.

This becomes obvious when we consider, for example, a pearl you find on the beach.

You have expended zero labor to cultivate the pearl. You've simply stumbled onto a pearl. And it is worth far more than a potato someone planted, cultivated, and then picked. Why?

The labor theory of value cannot answer that simple question.

This question led to the second theory of value: the so-called "subjective theory of value." This theory was created by the so-called Austrian School of Economics, which included major economic thinkers like Carl Menger, Eugen von Bohm-Bawerk, and Friedrich Wieser. Their theory was simple: The value of a good, product, or service is *whatever you are willing to pay for it*. That's why it's *subjective*: It's up to you. In this view, it doesn't matter how much labor was put into a good, product, or service. You don't care about that. You have literally *never* bought a shoe and thought, "Hey, how many hours of labor went into this shoe?" You have *never* bought a potato and thought, "I wonder how much the mortgage was on the farmland upon which this was grown, how many workers were employed at the farm, how much the gasoline cost to truck this potato to the local grocery store."

You have thought, very simply, "Is the price of this potato what I'm willing to pay? Or not?"

This idea—now obvious to nearly everyone—was not particularly obvious when it was first proposed by the Austrians. It seems counterintuitive, after all, because we value *our own labor* in a certain way. But the reality is that our labor is only worth what others are willing to pay for it.

The most famous example of the subjective theory of value is the so-called water/diamonds problem—a variation on the pearl/potato question. Why is a diamond worth more than a glass of water? Obviously, water is vital to life: Without it, you die. A diamond isn't just nonvaluable in most circumstances—it is the *definitionally* useless: You wear it because it's beautiful, not because it adds utility to your life.

So why will people pay millions of dollars for diamonds but then be shocked by the $10 price of a bottle of water?

The answer lies in *marginal utility*.

Marginal utility is a fancy way of saying that when you buy a good, product, or service, you're assessing the value of the thing in front of you, not *all the things with the same name*. Sure, water *in the aggregate* is more important than diamonds, and thus more valuable *in the aggregate*: All the potable water on earth would be worth tens of trillions of dollars, while all the diamonds on earth would be worth a fraction of that. But when you buy a glass of water, you're not buying all the water on earth: You're buying a glass of water. And there is a *lot of water* on earth. Which means that you could just as easily buy a different glass of water than the one you're currently buying. There are far fewer diamonds, particularly ones of the clarity and cut you may be looking for. That's why diamonds are more expensive than water.

But you could easily imagine a situation where the value of a glass of water would be higher than that of a diamond. If you were dying of thirst in the desert, you would undoubtedly pay a *lot more* for that glass of water than for a diamond.

In short, you're paying for the utility of an item *on the margin*. Hence the phrase *marginal utility*.

This theory—the subjective theory of value, the idea that an object is worth what it is worth to you, at this moment—is the actual basis of functional human economic relations. It is why you and I must agree on a price, rather than me simply cramming down an "objective" price on you. It is why prices change over time. It is why markets must *remain free*, rather than prices set by a centralized power: No centralized power on earth has the ability to decide for you or for the aggregate of humanity what a good, product, or service is "worth."

That can only be determined by the interplay of individual human beings themselves.

It can only be determined by free markets.

Free markets allow the entirety of humanity to weigh in on the relative merit of—well, anything. They are the most perfect system of evaluating merit ever evolved. This is why true meritocracies rely so deeply on free markets.

The Utilitarian Case for Free Markets

As we've seen, for thousands of years, all the requisite materials for computers and spacecraft, for MRI imaging and penicillin were available to mankind. Human nature didn't fundamentally change—the IQ of mankind has risen over time, but there is no reason to think that Aristotle would have felt out of place at the Massachusetts Institute of Technology, if he'd been educated in the same environments as other MIT students.

Yet nothing happened, for thousands of years.

Then something wonderful happened: Free markets emerged, after centuries of gradual evolution and broadening of property rights.

And mankind was unshackled from the chains of economic tyranny.

The Lions were set loose.

Free markets do one thing better than any other system in human history: They incentivize innovation. And it is innovation that turns luxuries into everyday necessities, and makes even poor men rich by comparison with their ancestors.

One of the great myths of our time is that progress is built on the back of the wage-worker. Wage-workers certainly provide a valuable service—their labor is, of course, absolutely indispensable—but technological and material progress is built on the back of the entrepreneur, for it is the entrepreneur who risks it all to build something. As economist Joseph Schumpeter put it:

> [Entrepreneurial profit] is the expression of the value of what the entrepreneur contributes to production in exactly the same way that wages are the value expression of what the worker "produces." It is not a profit of exploitation any more than are wages.... Without development there is no profit, without profit no development ... it is the entrepreneur's action that creates most fortunes.[23]

Innovation relies on risk and reward. Those who voluntarily bear risks in the name of exploration must be rewarded for doing so—after all, it is they who absorb the costs of the risk. Entrepreneurs venture forth, bringing new ideas into the world ... and they fail far more often than they succeed. In order to incentivize such risk-taking, risk *must be rewarded*. The man who starts a business must first believe enough in his idea to risk his time. He obsesses over an idea, investigates it from every angle. He plans, he considers, he rejects, he plans again. Then he risks his capital, or the capital he can raise. He mortgages his house, takes out a loan, or receives an investment to be counted against his prospective business. Finally, he risks himself: He pours himself into the project, taking time from his family, risking his own mental and emotional well-being to roll the dice on his idea.

The successful innovator changes the world.

But free markets don't just create individual innovators. They create an endless *cascade* of innovation.

No one mind is capable of generating true innovation on a tabula rasa, a blank slate. Innovation requires understanding of the past; it often involves collaboration with others; it requires a feedback loop from consumers and producers—in short, innovation requires commerce between minds across time and space. The development of the personal computer, for example, didn't happen overnight: It took decades of incremental innovation over time. Historian Walter Isaacson begins his history of the digital revolution in *1840*. As he says, "The computer and the Internet are among the most important inventions of our era, but few people know who created them. They were not conjured up in a garret or garage by solo inventors suitable to be singled out on magazine covers or put into a pantheon with Edison, Bell, and Morse. Instead, most of the innovations of the digital age were done collaboratively."[24] This was one of Hayek's greatest ideas: the idea that information is decentralized. Knowledge, Hayek pointed out, "never exists in concentrated or integrated form but solely as the dispersed bits of incomplete and frequently contradictory knowledge which all the separate individuals possess."[25] Only when those individuals are put in contact with one another, allowed to trade ideas and goods and products and services, can true innovation happen.

The result is something spectacular: a virtuous cycle of innovation.

As Schumpeter explains, once the initial pioneers of entrepreneurship succeed, they are quickly followed by more:

> Others can then follow these pioneers, as they will clearly do under the stimulus of the success now attainable. Their success again makes it easier ... for more people to follow suit, until finally the innovation becomes familiar and the acceptance of it a matter of free choice.[26]

Now innovators begin working together, drawing from one another.

They can do this thanks to free markets.

When free markets are allowed to flourish, magic occurs.

This is how a product made in a hundred different countries arrives at your door inside of two days from Amazon Prime.

In his extraordinary essay "I, Pencil," economist Leonard E. Read studies the example of the titular pencil. Writing in first person, he contends, "I, Pencil, simple though I appear to be, merit your wonder and awe, a claim I shall attempt to prove. In fact, if you can understand me—no, that's too much to ask of anyone—if you can become aware of the miraculousness which I symbolize, you can help save the freedom mankind is so unhappily losing." What is that miraculousness? Pencils roll off the assembly line, they end up in our desks or backpacks, and they cost nearly nothing. Yet no single person on the planet can actually create a pencil.

In order to understand the miracle of what human innovation and freedom of commerce can create, Read traces the genealogy of a single pencil: cedar grown in Northern California and Oregon; mining of ore and making of steel in order to create the saw to cut down that cedar; growing of hemp to create the rope to bind the lumber; logging camps and all their accoutrements to house the men who cut down the cedar and ship it; rails and railroads to move the lumber; mills to cut and dry the cedar repeatedly, complete with all their antecedent machinery; the power plant that provides the electricity to run the mill; the pencil factory, where the pieces of wood are glued together over the graphite; graphite itself mined in Sri Lanka, with all the tools necessary to do the mining; mixing of that graphite with clay from Mississippi; animal fats used to create the mixture, from their various sources; the addition of wax from Mexico and lacquer from castor beans; the ferrule made from brass; the rubber from rapeseed oil from the Dutch East Indies mixed with sulfur chloride, pumice from Italy, and more.

As Read says, "millions of human beings have had a hand in my creation, no one of whom even knows more than a very few of the others." The miracle of this uncoordinated, complex and yet emergent process is greater even than the miracle of nature itself. "[T]he configuration of creative human energies—millions of tiny know-hows configurating naturally and spontaneously in response to human necessity and desire and in the absence of any human masterminding!"

Read's closing message is crucial: "Leave all creative energies uninhibited. Merely organize society to act in harmony with this lesson. Let society's legal apparatus remove all obstacles the best it can. Permit these creative know-hows freely to flow. Have faith that free men and women will respond to the Invisible Hand. This faith will be confirmed."[27]

Read's lesson has been amply proved across time and space.

Countries without a history of free markets, after adopting free-market principles, have prospered. Those that have rejected free-market principles have sunk into the economic mire. Octogenarian career-useless-person Senator Bernie Sanders writes, "The American economic system, with its excessive corporate greed and concentration of ownership and power, destroys anything that gets in its way in the pursuit of profits. It destroys the environment. It destroys our health. It destroys our democracy. It discards human beings without a second thought."[28] Yet precisely the opposite is true. Like Karl Marx raging against the phantom immiseration of the workers, Sanders is lying on behalf of a failed communist god: Free-market countries are *better* for the environment than their socialist competitors, *better* for health than their socialist competitors, *better* for labor than their socialist competitors.

Draw a line across the middle of the Korean Peninsula, and see the difference. Before the Korean War, there was no difference between North Koreans and South Koreans in terms of economic well-being. Since then, South Korea has gradually embraced free markets while North Korea has wallowed in the toxic stew of tyrannical socialism. The result: a gap in gross domestic product per capita of over $30,000. North Koreans, due to malnutrition, are reportedly up to three inches shorter on average than their genetically indistinguishable South Korean brethren.[29]

This is true everywhere free markets reign: Things get better and cheaper.

Consider, for example, light. Today we take for granted that we can flick on a switch and, for nearly nothing, illuminate the night. But of course, that wasn't always the case. As Nobel Prize–winning economist William Nordhaus points out, a hundred-watt incandescent bulb, left on for three hours, produces 1.5 million lumen-hours of light per year. That number of lumen hours would have required 17,000 candles in 1800, costing an average worker 1,000 hours. Today, thanks to technological innovation and increased prosperity, that same number of lumen hours cost the average worker 10 minutes of time in 1990.

As economist Marian Tupy says, "Relative to wages, everything has become less expensive, including gold, platinum and silver and oil and gas. What really is increasing over time is human productivity and human wages."[30] And as Tupy points out, global income per person was approximately $2 per day in the days of Caesar Augustus, and had only advanced to $2.80 per day by the presidency of Thomas

Jefferson 1,800 years later; today world GDP per capita is in excess of $13,000.[31]

All thanks to free markets.

RULE #3: THE PRIDE REQUIRES PUBLIC VIRTUE

A functional Pride requires more than free minds and free markets, however.

It also requires public virtue.

After all, there are those who cannot take care of themselves in any society: children, the mentally or physically ill, the temporarily indigent. The by-product of freedom in economics is prosperity—but the by-product of liberty in personal relationships is chaos. Virtue and duty to one's fellows are the prerequisite for a society that prizes liberty. Free markets embolden the hunters. But virtue provides the framework for warriors and weavers—those who defend our society and those who build its social fabric.

Adam Smith famously understood just this. In *The Theory on Moral Sentiments*, which predates *The Wealth of Nations* by nearly two decades, Smith posited that human beings exchanged regard and esteem in the same way they exchanged goods and services—that human beings sought more than mere wealth, but honor as well.

> Man naturally desires, not only to be loved, but to be lovely; or to be that thing which is the natural and proper object of love. He naturally dreads, not only to be hated, but to be hateful; or to be that thing which is the natural and proper object of hatred. He desires, not only praise, but praiseworthiness; or to

be that thing which, though it should be praised by nobody, is, however, the natural and proper object of praise. He dreads, not only blame, but blame-worthiness; or to be that thing which, though it should be blamed by nobody, is, however, the natural and proper object of blame.

Because human beings sought esteem, Smith suggested, they would act benevolently. Benevolence could not be "extorted by force"; it had to be voluntary, and would be rewarded by society. The truly benevolent, "[b]y being productive of the greatest good . . . are the natural and approved objects of the liveliest gratitude."[32]

Benevolence, in other words, produces its own form of meritocracy—in which merit is measured not purely in market terms, in dollars and cents, but in terms of earned social capital. This is why a teacher is no less meritorious than a billionaire, and may be *more* meritorious depending on the standard of measurement. The billionaire may have more dollars, but the teacher may have more gratitude.

This is why so many billionaires seek moral capital and not merely financial capital. "I believe the power to make money is a gift of God," said John J. Rockefeller, the richest individual in American history, "to be developed and used to the best of our ability for the good of mankind. Having been endowed with the gift I possess, I believe it is my duty to make money and still more money and to use the money I make for the good of my fellow man according to the dictates of my conscience."[33]

For centuries, true Lions have understood obligations to those who require help—not to Scavengers, who falsely claim a prerogative to the spoils of the Lions, but to the truly vulnerable. I have yet to meet a billionaire who objects to the idea that she ought to give charity to those who truly require it. It is not a coincidence that America, the most individualistic society in terms of markets, has also been the most privately charitable society in human history. Americans have traditionally understood that public virtue requires institutions within which to act—that signing a check isn't enough. The only way to ensure that the truly deserving receive help, rather than Scavengers, is by ensuring that everyone who receives help demonstrates a baseline commitment to the rules of the game.

Historically, this function was performed by families, churches, and social associations. Membership in such nongovernmental groups required a precommitment to the ideals of the group, an understanding of common cause, and a willingness to sacrifice on behalf of that common cause. If you wished to receive charity from a church, you had to be a member of the church and involve yourself in the life of the community; if you were a member of a family, you had obligations to the family that you had to fulfill in order to justify any supposed entitlements the family owed to you. These *intermediate institutions*, as philosopher Robert Nisbet called them, provided both the framework of obligations and the safety net for individuals.

And it worked. As Nisbet describes:

> We can ... use the family as an almost infallible touchstone of the material and cultural prosperity of a people. When it is strong, closely linked with private property, treated as the essential context of education in society, and its sanctity recognized by law and custom, the probability is extremely high that we shall find the rest of the social order characterized by that subtle but puissant fusion of stability and individual mobility which is the hallmark of great ages.[34]

The same was true of churches.

In certain places, it still is.

In our shul community, for example, if someone loses his job, the community quickly springs into action. A meal train comes together to ensure that the children have enough to eat; WhatsApp groups fill with community members seeking information about open jobs on behalf of the man; the shul may organize a charity fund to see the family through the difficult time. This typically continues until the man finds a job. The man, in turn, understands that when he has a job again, he will be contributing in precisely the same way—and because he knows all the people from whom he is receiving charity personally, he is loath to take advantage of his fellow community members.

America, as a country, has been characterized by its high levels of commitment to intermediate institutions—churches, social clubs, community institutions designed to help those in need. Tocqueville famously writes:

> Americans of all ages, all conditions, all minds constantly unite. Not only do they have commercial and industrial associations in which all take part, but they also have a thousand other kinds: religious, moral, grave, futile, very general and very particular, immense and very small; Americans use associations to give fêtes, to found seminaries, to build inns, to raise churches, to distribute books, to send missionaries to the antipodes; in this manner they create hospitals, prisons, schools. Finally, if it is a question of bringing to light a truth or developing a sentiment with the support of a great example, they associate. Everywhere that, at the head of a new undertaking, you see the government in France and a great lord in England, count on it that you will perceive an association in the United States.[35]

Intermediate institutions are *bargains between individuals that establish a network of commitments*. By contrast, governmental entitlement programs demand nothing from beneficiary recipients—and tend to promote a Scavenger mentality, in which those who cash the checks feel no obligation to maintain the social fabric. When government replaces intermediate institutions, intermediate institutions wither—and then, as public virtue falls by the wayside, tyranny grows to fill the gap.

Public virtue, then, and institutions that both value and incentivize it are indispensable to the maintenance of the Pride. No government can substitute for them. The bargain of the Pride is simple: If you wish to be a member, you must exhibit public virtue. Public virtue, in fact, is the indispensable bedrock of communal survival. As philosopher Alisdaire MacIntyre writes, "What matters at this stage is the construction of local forms of community within which civility and the intellectual and moral life can be sustained through the new dark ages which are already upon us."[36]

RULE #4: THE PRIDE IMPLEMENTS EQUAL RIGHTS UNDER LAW

It is not enough for free minds, free markets, and public virtue to exist.

Lions must also be protected by the system of law.

Every community has a hierarchy of power. In functional communities, as we've explored, the Lions are those with the most skill, utility, and commitment. Typically, such skill and utility come in a combination of attributes: mental agility, physical prowess, capacity for conflict resolution. In the most functional and durable communities, the Lions also have wisdom—and that wisdom leads them to principles of justice. After all, a Lion cannot hunt alone. He must have a Pride, and that Pride will only acquiesce in a particular hierarchy if the rules are predictable and fair.

Lions cannot be allowed to turn their productive leadership into tyranny.

That is indeed the tendency of those who become successful: It's often easier to rig the system in your own favor than to continue to play by the rules. It's why major business leaders cultivate political favor. It's why they engage lobbyists to quietly rewrite the rules of the game. And why they seek political power directly, thus enshrining their own domination.

If Lions establish tyranny, they become Scavengers: They abandon the fundamental principles of their own philosophy, and substitute instead a grasping, ugly philosophy that values power alone. Power does not necessarily corrupt, but the pure desire for power—the willingness to cling to power even when you do not merit it—corrupts absolutely. Such gluttony for power warps Lions into Scavengers.

And those Scavengers proceed to destroy everything.

It is simply not possible to create wealth in an environment in which your hard work, time, capital, and intellectual effort can be removed from you at will by an outside power. There is no reason for anyone to invest resources into building a house that can be burned down at any moment. In general, only the incentive of *keeping what you build* causes people to build things. Pure altruism on behalf of a collective never lasts long, and never extends to all of humanity. Eventually, abolishing private property ends with someone needing to point a gun at someone else and saying, "Build, or else." The absence of property rights first leads to impoverishment, as Lions cease to build; then the Scavengers employ violence to compel the Lions to do work they no longer wish to do.

Any nation that fails to protect property rights via rule of law damns its own population to poverty. Nobel Prize–winning economist Hernando de Soto spent decades examining underdeveloped economies in Latin America. One factor predominated over all others: lack of predictable and protectable property rights. People lived in shacks without owning the underlying land; they started illegal businesses. But those assets had no outside value: No one could pay value for the shacks without the underlying property rights, or buy an illegal business. Without "institutions that give life to capital," de Soto said, people end up in "cit[ies] of the dead—of dead capital, of assets that cannot be used to their fullest.... The formal property system is capital's hydroelectric plant. This is the place where capital is born."[37]

The rule of law is the seedbed of prosperity and decency.

So, how do we establish a system that prizes the rule of law?

In a functional Pride, there must be both internal and external checks on the Lions. Internal checks, in the West, have typically come in the form of religious obligations. Attempts to enshrine internal systems of virtue absent God have generally failed; that is the rationale behind Voltaire's famous epigram that if God didn't exist, it would be necessary to invent him. Traditionally, belief in biblical values provided an internal check—although in practice, an insufficient check—against the potential sins of the powerful. Above all kings is a King of Kings; above all laws is a Higher Law.

In the Bible, the king is commanded to write and carry around a copy of the Torah, to remind him of his obligations to God. In the prophetic tradition, prophets of the Lord are sent to chastise kings; the first Israelite king, Saul, is deposed by Samuel, prophet of the Lord, for his failures to listen to God's command, the kingdom ripped away from him.

British kings traditionally bound themselves to three Higher Laws: the pledge to provide peace for the Church of God and all the people; to forbid acts of robbery and violence; and to uphold both justice and mercy.

Theoretically, any governmental system could effectuate the rules of the pride. A good monarch could easily enforce free markets and protect intermediate institutions. So could an aristocracy, in theory.

In practice, however, well-governed societies recognize the innate frailties and temptations of mankind, and place external checks on those at the top of the system of power. After all, centralized power tends to thwart meritocracy: The temptation toward abuse of that power in favor of friends and associates is simply too great. This is what the Founding Fathers recognized: Checks and balances were the best way to prevent a natural meritocracy from calcifying into a permanent, corrupt power structure. As James Madison put it in *Federalist* No. 51:

> Ambition must be made to counteract ambition.... If men were angels, no government would be necessary. If angels were to govern men, neither external nor internal controls on government would be necessary. In framing a government which is to be administered by men over men, the great difficulty lies in this: you must first enable the government to control the governed; and in the next place oblige it to control itself.[38]

The process leading to the checks and balances of modern republican government was long and winding. It began with a struggle between the elites in England, where lords sought a balance of power from the king in the Magna Carta; eventually that balance of power would manifest in a powerful parliament, a centuries-long evolution that culminated in the Glorious Revolution, which "strengthened and rationalized property rights, improved financial markets, undermined state-sanctioned monopolies in foreign trade, and removed the barriers to the expansion of industry ... [and] made the political system open and responsive to the economic needs and aspirations of society."[39]

The US Constitution was the apex of that process: a system designed to protect individual rights from mob rule, and to protect the people from a government strong enough to crush them. As Ayn Rand notes:

> It took centuries of intellectual, philosophical development to achieve political freedom.... The individual was not left at the mercy of his neighbors or his leaders: the Constitutional system of checks and balances was scientifically devised to protect him from both.[40]

The eventual explosion of democratic republicanism, complete with checks and balances, has made the world inordinately richer and better.

The night is sweltering, but the crowd buzzes with excitement.

We're in the Rio Grande Valley, on the border of Texas and Mexico, in a city of 142,000 called McAllen. The population is 87 percent Hispanic, according to the last census; the median income for a family is $50,000.

This is a blue-collar town, and it's filled with blue-collar people.

And they're here, at the University Draft House, a thousand strong, waiting to hear me introduce Senator Ted Cruz, who is in a tough re-election battle with Democrat Colin Allred.

It would be difficult to imagine a setting more different from the stately aesthetic of the Capitol: a made-over fire station, the smells of burgers and beer, the rowdy atmosphere. But it's the people at University Draft House who represent the foundation for the classical architecture in the People's House.

On the surface, I don't share much in common with the people who have come out tonight to hear me speak. I'm an Orthodox Jew; they're largely Catholic. I have an Ivy League educational background; most of these people never went to college.

But we do have one thing in common, and it's the most important thing: a common vision for what's wrong with the nation, and what it takes to fix it. They're here because they're distraught about the state of their country: about a wide-open border; about the dearth of economic opportunity in a stagnating economy; about the ongoing assault on traditional values.

As I emerge from a room in the back of the facility, the crowd roars.

They want a say in how their government is run.

They want their voices heard.

They want the rules of the Pride to be maintained. In fact, they demand it.

They demand that their freedom of mind be protected. They want the opportunity to speak freely, to attend the church of their choice, to associate with their friends, families, coreligionists, fellow Americans.

They demand that free markets be preserved. They understand that the opportunity to build generational wealth on behalf of their children and grandchildren rests on private property, not the empty promises of politicians who say they will take from some to give to others.

They demand that public virtue be upheld. These are not prudes or puritans, not the "bitter clinger" of Barack Obama. They know that the vitality of their community rests on charity and faith, on a thriving social fabric than cannot be replaced by a do-gooder government that offers tyranny with an unctuous smile.

And they demand that every American be treated equally under the law. They know that any government that seeks to benefit one group at the expense of another is no government worth its name—that double standards in law mean no standards at all.

They want the same things that citizens all over the continent want. Over the course of the 2024 campaign, I have campaigned in Ohio, Wisconsin, Pennsylvania, Montana, Nevada, and Texas. The crowds varied in terms of size and race and age. But they all wanted the same things: the rules of the Pride applied.

This is what America looks like.

These are Lions.

And those Lions are the result of a system of rules and institutions unique to the West. That system generates Lions from Putnam County to Las Vegas; from Pittsburgh to Oshkosh. In his first inaugural address, Ronald Reagan spoke of the Lions:

> It is time for us to realize that we're too great a nation to limit ourselves to small dreams.... We have every right to dream heroic dreams. Those who say that we're in a time when there are not heroes, they just don't know where to look. You can see heroes every day going in and out of factory gates. Others, a handful in number, produce enough food to feed all of us and then the world beyond. You meet heroes across a counter, and they're on both sides of that counter. There are entrepreneurs

with faith in themselves and faith in an idea who create new jobs, new wealth and opportunity. They're individuals and families whose taxes support the government and whose voluntary gifts support church, charity, culture, art, and education. Their patriotism is quiet, but deep. Their values sustain our national life.

Those values—the values of the Lions—can sustain us still.
But only if we fight for them.
And we *will* have to fight for them.
Because the Scavengers are on the move.

CHAPTER FOUR

THE WAY OF THE SCAVENGER

OXFORD, ENGLAND

We see them.

We see the rivers of humanity, their fists raised, their flags of third-world countries and terror groups held aloft, the hatred in their eyes, climbing our monuments and defacing them, ripping down our flags and replacing them with their own.

We hear them chant for our eradication, their screaming voices raised in ecstatic frenzy, the stamping of their feet as they march in unison against us.

We feel their venom, their senseless and ceaseless animosity, their blame, their shame, their rage.

They are all around us.

These are the Scavengers.

The Scavengers are those who produce nothing, and demand everything.

The Scavengers are those who demand as their right that which has been produced by others; who blame their own miseries, in free societies, on "systems of power" that supposedly rob them of autonomy; who claim that failure is a virtue and success a sin.

They are creatures of envy.

They are creatures of *ressentiment*.

They are creatures of destruction.

Last night, I traveled to the Oxford Union, a debating society established in 1823, to do an event.

I had been scheduled, originally, to travel to Oxford to discuss American politics—social conservatism and gay marriage, tax rates and the Second Amendment. But with Israel now targeting Hamas military targets—and with Hamas hiding behind their own civilians in order to maximize civilian casualties so that softheaded media would aim their ire at Israel—the topic would undoubtedly turn to the Middle East.

Given the widespread reports of anti-Semitism in London—given the pictures of hundreds of thousands of Hamas fellow travelers mobbing the London Bridge—I had some trepidation about visiting. I decided to go anyway.

Oxford is the oldest university in England, which is to say in the Anglo-American world; teaching began at the university as early as 1096, just three decades after the Norman invasion of the British Isles. Famous Oxford teachers and alumni include Roger Bacon, Sir Walter Raleigh, John Donne, Thomas Hobbes, Samuel Johnson, Adam Smith, Jonathan Swift, Edward Gibbon, John Locke, and Cardinal John Henry Newman, among others.[1]

The campus is, of course, indescribably beautiful.

Its Gothic and Baroque architectures are so embedded in the latent consciousness of the West that it feels almost cliché. Before the event, staff gave us a tour of the Old Library, a structure erected in 1857, originally as the debating chamber at the university. Above the shelves of books, murals of scenes from Arthurian legend line the walls. One of the painters, Dante Gabriel Rossetti, describes his contribution in an 1858 letter commemorating his depiction of Sir Lancelot, barred from the Holy Grail by his love for Queen Guinevere:

> My own subject (for each of us has as yet done only one) is Sir Lancelot prevented by his sin from entering the chapel of the Sancgrael. He has fallen asleep before the shrine full of angels, & between him & it, rises in his dream the image of Queen Guenevere, the cause of all. She stands gazing at him with her arms extended in the branches of an apple tree.[2]

Just a few short blocks from the library, set in hedge overrun with leaves, is a marker. It carries an inscription, which reads simply:

> NEAR TO THIS SITE
> STOOD THE KING'S HOUSES
> LATER KNOWN AS
> BEAUMONT PALACE
> KING RICHARD I
> WAS BORN HERE IN 1157
> AND KING JOHN IN 1167

We are in the beating heart of historic Britain.

And as I learned last night, the heart has been ripped from Britain's body.

As we knew from communications prior to the event, the president of the Oxford Union was antipathetic to my worldview. That much became clear throughout the process of event planning, and was no great surprise. She even attempted to bar me from giving an opening statement, even though such opening statements were common practice at Oxford Union (even highly respected porn star Stormy Daniels gave an opening statement when she spoke there).

I began with an opening statement anyway, in which I showed photos of the atrocities perpetrated by Hamas, and pointed out that siding with Hamas was evil.

Then, student after student sided with Hamas.

The hatred in the room was palpable.

Student after student called for Israel to be destroyed utterly. Student after student made excuses for Hamas's murderous rampage.

After an hour of this, I gave a closing statement.

"I think tonight we've seen some evidence of people obscuring some clear moral differentiation between the targeted burning of babies in their homes in front of their mothers by shoving them into an oven," I said, "and people attempting to kill terrorists who are themselves putting civilians in harm's way in violation of the rules of war and the Geneva Conventions. And if you're one of the people who's making this sort of moral equivalence I ask for you to check your own heart. And if you're one of the people watching people making this moral equivalence and being convinced by the supposed complexity of the issue, I ask for you to check your brain."

I walked from the hall, tense with adrenaline. My personal security team would later inform me that the event was one of the most fraught they had ever attended.

As protesters outside chanted slogans in favor of Hamas, the litany of rage went on: radical Muslims damning the West and Israel for their supposed settler colonialism, leftists joining in the melee, all boiling together into one frothing stew of hatred. All in the birthplace of Richard Lionheart, leader of the Third Crusade to liberate Jerusalem from Muslim invasion.

Now the invasion has come home, aided by the West itself.

THE IMPULSE OF THE SCAVENGER

There are subterranean rivers—passions—that flow within the human heart. They speed and rush and overrun their banks; they are constantly ready to break free, flooding society at large.

They are dangerous and they are terrible and they are awesome.

Civilization is the art of channeling those passions productively.

Through civilization, we transform passions into assets. We convert fires that could lead to deadly sin into combustion engines for productivity.

Thus selfishness becomes interest; interest is checked against interest, generating freedom and democracy.

Pride becomes ambition; ambition spurs us to achievement.

Lust becomes love; monogamy builds the family.

Wrath becomes righteous indignation; that rightcous indignation spurs us to honorable action.

Gluttony becomes acquisitiveness; that acquisitiveness lies at the source of innovation.

Sloth becomes leisure; leisure lies at the heart of play.

The chief moral mechanism by which we channel our passions is by *decentering* ourselves, and by recentering a Higher Law. We realize that we are not the center of the universe, and that our passions are only some among many. We abide by the biblical dictate that every man is made in the image of God, and that our neighbor's passions are no less vital than our own.

We are made equal before God.

In that equality, moreover, we sublimate our individual passions to a greater whole. That greater whole is the *community*; a functioning community treats its citizens as equal in moral importance, with all the rights to which they are entitled, so long as those citizens channel their passions rather than giving way to them.

A properly constituted community channels passions into assets.

But there is one passion that cannot be transmuted by civilization. It is a universal acid, eating through civilization itself, destroying the mechanisms by which passions become assets, and transforming those assets back into passions.

That passion is envy.

Adam Smith defines envy as "that passion which views with malignant dislike the superiority of those who are really entitled to all the superiority they possess."[3]

Envy is pure poison.

Through envy, interests become selfishness; ambition becomes unearned pride; love becomes lust; acquisitiveness becomes gluttony; leisure becomes sloth.

Envy springs from a simple, disastrously wrong premise: that the world ought to conform to my desires. Thus any denial of my passions—any transformation of my passions into assets—is a reflection of injustice. Were the world less unfair, I would have all I want.

And the world *is* unfair.

So the world must be transformed. The highest must be brought low. The powerful must be made powerless. The successful must be dragged into the dust.

Envy is the animating passion of the Scavengers.

But the Scavengers must somehow justify that passion. After all, it would not do for them to simply acknowledge that envy drives the savagery in which the Scavengers delight. And so Scavengers weave a justification around their envy.

That justification is simple: that Scavengers are not merely envious Lions.

In reality, the Scavengers claim, they are not *actually* Scavengers at all. The Scavenger claims he is merely a victimized Lion. The Scavenger believes that his envy is not envy, but a claim of justice.

The Scavenger believes that he is, in fact, the *true* Lion.

That those who appear to be lions are, in reality, the *true* scavengers.

The Scavenger claims that his own failures are, in fact, the fault of the pseudo-Lions—usurpers who have exploited them and laid them low. That while he, the Scavenger, might appear to be a Scavenger right now, he is actually a hidden king, robbed of his birthright by the *true* Scavenger—a Scavenger now masquerading as a Lion.

The Scavenger claims that a Great Reversal has taken place. That the institutions around us are a lie, designed to perpetuate that Reversal. That the rules governing civilization are merely power constructs, created to suppress the true Lions—the people who now clamor for the uprooting of civilization.

The Scavenger claims that he and others like him will rise up again, and that in pursuit of that rising, all is justified.

Thus envy is transformed into virtue.

This is a lie—but it is an attractive lie. In fact, it is an entire attractive philosophy: the philosophy of *ressentiment*.

Ressentiment is merely envy distilled.

The basic concept of *ressentiment* is simple: People project their own inferiority onto something else—another person, a broader system. Friedrich Nietzsche suggested that *ressentiment* would manifest as construction of a slave morality by which power would itself be seen as evil. In ancient times, Nietzsche says, people admired those who were beautiful, noble, good, and powerful; those who are filled with *ressentiment* hate those qualities precisely because they lack them, and thus they create an alternative morality turning the world upside down. In Nietzsche's incorrect interpretation of Judaism, this was Judaism's chief sin: "It was the Jews who, with awe-inspiring consistency, dared to invert the aristocratic value-equation (good = noble = powerful = beautiful = happy = beloved of God) and to hang on to the inversion with their teeth . . ., saying 'the wretched alone are the good; the poor, impotent, lowly alone are the good; the suffering, deprived, sick, ugly alone are pious, alone are blessed by God.'"[4] According to Nietzsche, Christianity then perfected this logic and brought it to the world.

Of course, the Bible says no such thing: Far from worshipping weakness, the Bible requires worship of an all-powerful God. The Bible states that might and right aren't necessarily connected, and that only right matters—but the Bible *never* suggests that success in and of itself ought to mark the powerful as sinful, or that failure ought to mark the powerless as righteous. "You shall not be partial to the poor," says Deuteronomy, "or defer to the great, but in righteousness shall you judge your neighbor." The Bible is replete with reminders that man's failures are all too often self-generated.

But there *is* a philosophy that elevates those who fail at the expense of those who succeed, even in a free and fair system—and that prescribes total societal tyranny in order to reverse the consequences of the meritocracy.

THE PHILOSOPHY OF THE SCAVENGER

The West has been infiltrated with a sick philosophy.

Like the philosophy of the Lion, that philosophy isn't truly held forth as a philosophy—it's more of an impulse. Few Scavengers spend time thinking about the roots of their actions. In fact, if they admitted to the true root of their action—*ressentiment*—they would have to admit that they were driven by the basest motivation. That is precisely what they will never do. Instead they must lie, craft entire identities around pretended righteousness. They act adamantly and insistently—and sometimes violently. Ask them their philosophy, and they may spew a few bromidic slogans. But they know, deep in their hearts, what it is they believe, even if they cannot articulate it.

It does not take a philosopher to be a Scavenger.

It requires only seething hatred of the Lion and his ways.

The philosophy of the Lion, as we've explained, contains three central principles:

1. There is a master plan, a Logos behind the universe.
2. You are made in the image of God: you are a creative, choosing being with autonomy and power. The choice of triumph or sin is your own. The choice of knowledge or ignorance is yours. Responsibility is yours.
3. You have true and meaningful moral duties in this world—duties that derive not from your feelings, but from God, from age-old civilizational traditions, and from the dictates of reason. Fulfillment of these duties brings meaning and purpose to life. Failure to fulfill these duties brings misery.

The philosophy of the Scavenger disdains these principles. Instead, it offers its own competing three central principles:

1. There is no master plan behind the universe. The world is a purposeless place, and all morals and civilizations are merely guises for power.
2. Your failures are a result of one of these corrupt power systems. The world is a Great Conspiracy, and you are its victim.
3. Violence is the proper response to the Great Conspiracy against you.

If there is no master plan behind the universe, then there can be no independent justification of any system; power isn't just everything, it's the only thing.

If power is the only thing, then your failures aren't your fault—they're the fault of the corrupt system. You are being exploited, and you are a victim. The greater your failure, the greater your oppression.

The more you fail—and definitionally, are oppressed—the greater the justification for your violence.

These principles, when taken in tandem, provide a permission framework for true evil.

The First Principle: The World Is Defined by Power Dynamics

As we have seen, the biblical worldview—the worldview that has shaped our civilization of Lions—says that the world was created with purpose.

Scavengers believe, however, that the world is a cruel and purposeless place.

They believe that there is no logic to the universe—that the idea of a good God, who creates human beings out of love, is a cruel lie. Religious belief in a logical universe is actually a guise for cruel systems of power seeking to perpetuate themselves. As Karl Marx put it in his *Critique of Hegel's Philosophy of Right*:

> Religious suffering is at one and the same time the expression of real suffering and a protest against real suffering. Religion is the sigh of the oppressed creature, the heart of a heartless world and the soul of soulless conditions. It is the opium of the people. The abolition of religion as the illusory happiness of the people is the demand for their real happiness.[5]

In reality, according to Marx and his ideological allies, the world has no internal structure or logic. Man is alone in the universe, and is at best equipped only with the power to remake himself over and over again. All systems we see are therefore the products of the winners, who have exerted their power over the losers.

There are no moral systems, just power systems.

There is no truth, merely power.

There is no knowledge, merely power.

In the view of the Scavengers, we swim in a sea of power, expressing itself in a variety of forms and fashions. Our perception of reality itself is merely a reflection of power dynamics. In the words of Michel Foucault:

> We must cease once and for all to describe the effects of power in negative terms: it "excludes," it "represses," it "censors," it "abstracts," it "masks," it "conceals." In fact power produces; it

produces reality; it produces domains of objects and rituals of truth. The individual and the knowledge that may be gained of him belong to this production.[6]

There is good news, however, for the Scavenger: While the world may be governed by power, you can *seize power yourself*. In fact, that is what makes you most alive and human: seizing "your power," defining "your truth," without reference to morality. Nietzsche calls this phenomenon the "will to power" and says that it is both natural and unavoidable: "life itself is *essentially* appropriation, injury, overpowering of what is alien and weaker; suppression, hardness, imposition of one's own forms, incorporation and at least, at its mildest, exploitation...." The reality of life, Nietzsche suggests, is an "incarnate will to power," a necessity to "grow, spread, seize, become predominant—not from any morality or immorality but because it is *living* and because life simply *is* will to power."[7]

And power can be used for anything, since morality is a human invention.

As existentialist Jean-Paul Sartre put it:

Nowhere is it written that the Good exists, that we must be honest, that we must not lie; because the fact is we are on a plane where there are only men.... If existence really does precede essence, there is no explaining things away by reference to a fixed and given human nature. In other words, there is no determinism, man is free, man is freedom.[8]

This may sound inspiring.
Actually, it's evil.

If we make our own morality—and if we are free to define ourselves and the world around us—then any exercise of power is self-justifying. One need not appeal to right in order to excuse the rule of might, since there *is no right*, only might.

Which is precisely what Scavengers argue on their own behalf.

In fact, this is the argument of the snake in the Garden of Eden.

At the beginning of the book of Genesis, God creates man "in His image"—that is, with creative capacity and free will—and places him in the garden of Eden. God fills the garden with every sort of delight: Every tree that was pleasing to see, with fruit that was good to taste; the garden was watered by a river sourced in its center. And God places man in the garden, to "work it and to guard it."

But man is deceived by the argument of the Scavenger—the snake.

In the Genesis account, Eve, Adam's newly-created wife, meets the snake, the wiliest of creatures. The snake then spells out a conspiracy theory: In reality, God only wants to prevent Adam and Eve from eating from the tree so that God can maintain His mastery of the universe. "Did God really say: You shall not eat of any tree of the garden? . . . You are not going to die. God knows that as soon as you eat of it your eyes will be opened and you will be like gods, knowing good and evil."

In Milton's *Paradise Lost*, he characterizes the snake's—Satan's—argument thus:

Why then was this forbid?
Why, but to awe;
Why, but to keep ye low and ignorant, His worshippers?[9]

And Eve falls for the trick.

She believes the conspiracy: She and Adam are not the masters of their fates, but pawns being manipulated by an all-powerful Creator.

God is not moral; God is only powerful.

If only she strikes back at God by eating of the tree and convincing Adam to do the same, she and Adam will become powerful too. They can then redesign the garden.

And so Adam and Eve are thrown out of Eden. They are faced with the reality of a cruel and pitiless natural world, so different from the garden in which God placed them. They must learn responsibility, even in the face of hardship. Adam must learn to work the land, to master the truth of cause and effect, to earn his bread by the sweat of his brow; Eve must learn that the natural world is filled with pain and injustice, but that she must persevere anyway.

The lesson of the biblical narrative is clear: Our sins are our responsibility. Our failures are our own. But according to the Scavengers, the snake—Satan—was right.

It is no surprise that so many modern critics characterize Satan as the hero of *Paradise Lost*—that his proclamation that it is "better to reign in Hell than serve in Heaven" is an act of bravery, worthy of admiration. Romantic poet Percy Bysshe Shelley wrote, "Milton's Devil as a moral being is as far superior to his God as one who perseveres in some purpose which he has conceived to be excellent in spite of adversity and torture."[10]

It matters not that, absent God, all live in Hell.

All that matters is who rules.

The Second Principle: Your Failure Is Evidence of Your Victimhood

In the worldview of the Scavenger, failure means that someone has oppressed you.

According to the Scavenger, the only reason you failed is that you were oppressed by a person, a community, or a system. If you weren't oppressed, you would not have failed. The greater your failure, the deeper your oppression.

All failure—all disparity between winners and losers—is the result of discrimination.

This peculiar idea rests on a clear fallacy: that all human beings are born equal in their qualities and capabilities, or at least can be made so by proper systems. If this is the case—if human beings are all blank slates waiting to be imprinted by systems, equivalent in their talents and facilities—then any inequality is a sign of inequity embedded in systems. Upholding any system that perpetuates such disparities makes us complicit in such inequity. In the words of *White Fragility* author Robin DiAngelo, professor at the University of Washington: "if we truly believe that all humans are equal, then disparity in condition can only be the result of systemic discrimination."[11]

If, as DiAngelo says, we believe that all human beings are equal, and that disparity is a result of discrimination, then we can immediately judge whether a system is fair or not by its outcome. Unequal outcomes? Unfair systems.

Because meritocracies inherently distinguish between those who are more and less meritorious—that is what they are designed to do—they result in winners and losers. But if the very presence of winners and losers discredits a system as unfair, then meritocracy is inherently unfair.

In this view, there is no meritocracy: There are only rules rigged for the benefit of one party or another. Harvard philosopher Michael Sandel, for example, argues against a meritocracy: "Meritocracy isn't a remedy to inequality but its justification. Since it's assumed that social mobility can be achieved through work, then everyone deserves the place they end up in. But we can clearly see that this doesn't work."[12] Because, as Sandel points out, not everyone has the same opportunities—because of the lack of cosmic justice—Sandel recommends a top-down redistribution of resources by the wisest, all in the name of rectifying the natural inequalities between human beings.[13]

Sandel isn't alone in his flawed moral design. He follows in the footsteps of John Rawls, who distinguished between "fair equality of opportunity" and "formal equality of opportunity." Formal equality of opportunity—meaning equal rights under law and equal application of the law—was insufficient, in Rawls's view, since some people would be born into different circumstances, which means that those people would be inherently victimized by the system from birth. *Fair* equality of opportunity, by contrast, would work to cancel out those differences by benefiting those born into lesser circumstances.[14] Justice, in this view, would only be obtained by seeking cosmic justice on behalf of the less fortunate.

The philosophy of Sandel and Rawls isn't merely wrong.

It's dangerous.

It's dangerous because generally, the critique of meritocracy extends to a further argument: that meritocracy is *designed and maintained in order to be unfair*. And, as Thomas Sowell writes, "history shows how dangerous it can be, to a whole society, to automatically and incessantly attribute statistical differences in outcomes to malevolent actions against the less successful."[15]

That is precisely what the Scavengers posit: that if they fail, it is only because they are victims of purposeful oppression, systems designed *specifically* to hurt them. Are they failures? If so, their very failure is evidence of their victimhood at the hands of a Great Conspiracy.

This idea—that the presence of winners and losers in society is de facto evidence of an evil system, maintained and preserved by evil people—can be termed the Great Conspiracy Theory.

The Great Conspiracy Theory is common across societies. As philosopher Karl Popper writes:

> [T]he conspiracy theory of society ... is the view that an explanation of a social phenomenon consists in the discovery of the men or groups who are interested in the occurrence of this phenomenon (sometimes it is a hidden interest which has first to be revealed), and who have planned and conspired to bring it about. ... The belief in the Homeric gods whose conspiracies explain the history of the Trojan War is gone. The gods are abandoned. But their place is filled by powerful men or groups—sinister pressure groups whose wickedness is responsible for all the evils we suffer from—such as the Learned Elders of Zion, or the monopolists, or the capitalists, or the imperialists.[16]

Now, the Great Conspiracy Theory is enervating. It suggests that no matter how hard you work, no matter how rational and well calibrated your decisions, you will fail—because the system is out to get you. And if you disagree, you are likely *part of the system.*

It is worth examining how the Great Conspiracy Theory gains popularity.

The process begins with Just Asking Questions.

We have all been taught that we ought to be skeptical of received wisdom, that we ought to ask difficult questions. And that is certainly true. *Of course* we ought to ask questions.

But the purpose of a question is to *find an answer*.

Those who Just Ask Questions aren't actually interested in answers. Precisely the opposite. They are interested in justifying their particular Great Conspiracy Theory by discrediting those who actually *do* seek answers. Those who ask questions in order to obtain answers and solutions strengthen society; those who ask questions merely in order to tear away at the credibility of the institutions are Scavengers.

Just Asking Questions is an easy strategy for scavenging demagogues.

It begins by *implying* a Great Conspiracy Theory.

Is the earth flat? *The scientific authorities are lying to you.*

Was the moon landing real? *Your government will falsify anything, including one of the most viewed events in the history of the planet.*

Who was *really* behind the killing of JFK? *There must have been a group of powerful people who decided to assassinate the president, thus ushering in a new era in America of centralized power.*

Is America run by lizard people? *You can't trust any of your leaders.*

Do the Jews run the banking system? *There is a group of sinister outsiders who are utilizing the methodologies of power to subjugate you.*

These are all questions with definite, provable answers (the earth isn't flat, America's moon landing was real, JFK was shot by Lee Harvey Oswald, the United States isn't run by lizard people, and the 15 million Jews on planet earth do not control the global banking system). But these questions aren't designed to elicit answers. They are designed to obscure them, in order to reach the conclusion that *you can't trust the system*—in this case scientists, NASA, the CIA, Congress, or the banking system.

Once the Question has been asked—but never answered—the next step is pseudo-ignorance. When told that, for example, Lee Harvey Oswald shot JFK, you simply explain that you're no expert on the topic—you just know that you're being lied to by *someone*. You don't need evidence of lies, of course. You can rely on *your gut*. You've got *common sense*.

Hey, you aren't purporting to *know the answers*.

You just know that the answers you've been given are *insufficient*.

What makes them insufficient? That you don't believe them.

Your suspicions haven't been quelled, you see. And goodness knows, you would *love* to know the answers to these questions. But you just haven't been given satisfying answers by *those in power*.

Right-wing host Tucker Carlson, for example, revels in such posturing. After implying the possibility of a conspiracy by the government to—of all things—raise egg prices, this host unleashed the following stew of pseudo-ignorance and suspicion:

> We don't know. But we should tell you because again, no one else seems to be keeping track of this . . . we're agnostic on this, but we figured we would do a little poking. And they said they've looked into it too, and their feed is not the problem. And that may absolutely be true. We don't know. What we did notice, though, was that the explanation was more than enough for most media companies. . . .

This obviously isn't a search for an answer. It's an attack on the credibility of anyone who doesn't believe in the Great Chicken Conspiracy

Theory. Mere failure to buy into the idea that there is a Great Chicken Conspiracy makes you complicit in the Great Chicken Conspiracy.

This seems idiotic. But it *does* work. It works because few people are capable of seeing through pseudo-ignorance. We are all trained to believe that the greatest sin is arrogance—if a man claims ignorance, we tend to honor his claims and give him credit for humility. Those who Just Ask Questions weaponize that tendency against those of decent heart: They pretend they have no idea what they are talking about, when they most certainly do. Those who Just Ask Questions aren't children seeking answers; they are adults avoiding them. They cloak themselves in ignorance in order to promote certain perverse ideas, *not* to seek answers.

All of this leads to the third step in Just Asking Questions: the claim that anyone who objects to Just Asking Questions isn't just wrong—they're part of an active cover-up. Those who oppose conspiracy theories are *all a part of the conspiracy theory*.

Now, this part of the Just Asking Questions typically requires outright dishonesty. It requires that actual substantive criticisms of conspiracy theorists be derided as censorious and tyrannical. Those who Just Ask Questions, you see, are all part of an alliance, telling forbidden truths. They take flak only because they are "over the target." Thus the career-long conspiracy theorist Alex Jones—who has bombastically posited that the government's control of the weather has caused specific floods; that more than one of his political opponents control pedophilic sex rings; that the Sandy Hook shooting was staged; and that 9/11 was government-initiated—is actually a martyred possible "prophet," in Carlson's words:

> Alex Jones, Prophet. Not Conspiracy Nut, Prophet. But when you dig into Alex Jones's predictions, they are so spot-on that

it's remarkable. How does he do this? We're guessing there's a spiritual sensitivity to Alex Jones. Maybe that's his secret? He was displaying this years before the average person in this country even thought about matters like that.

Yes, it turns out that the more conspiracy theories you propose, the more you are targeted—because the truth cannot be allowed to get out there! Controversy becomes, in and of itself, a sign of truth.

Conspiracism, of course, is a bipartisan drug.

The entire lie of wokeness, for example—the conspiracy theory that racial discrepancies in American life are due to systemic American racism—is predicated on precisely the same strategies. First, Just Ask the Question: Why do black Americans *really* earn less than white Americans? Then, when confronted with facts—such as the disparity between black and white households with regard to family structure, rates of criminal arrest, educational attainment, and career choice—plead pseudo-ignorance: Hey, you can't label the precise law responsible for economic disparities, but you *know* something is wrong! Finally, identify those who deny that America is systemically racist as part of the conspiracy—they themselves are part of the racist infrastructure. When Nikole Hannah-Jones of *The New York Times* posited in her *1619 Project* that the American founding revolved around preservation of slavery, and when she was thoroughly debunked by historians of various political persuasions, she used precisely this tactic: "LOL. Right, because white historians have produced truly objective history."[17]

This tactic is indeed quite effective.

The question is *why*.

The answer lies in what philosopher Alisdaire MacIntyre termed *emotivism*, the argument that your opponent's opposition lies not in true philosophical difference, but in *secret motivation*: "the doctrine that all evaluative judgments and more specifically all moral judgments are nothing but expressions of preference, expressions of attitude or feeling, insofar as they are moral or evaluative in character."[18]

People don't disagree with you because they have a different opinion, but because they are *seeking to harm you*.

This is a terrible argument—it's actually not an argument at all, but an act of emotional manipulation. As McIntyre says, "emotivism entails the obliteration of the genuine distinction between manipulative and non-manipulative social relations."[19] In essence, discussion requires trust: It requires the trust that your opponent is not arguing in "bad faith," simply attempting any emotional trick or gambit to win. When social fabric decays, emotivism becomes commonplace: You don't trust your neighbor, and so you assume that he must be saying something to forward his own power.

Scavengers live on such emotivism.

It is their lifeblood.

Emotivism provides the framework for their Great Conspiracy Theory—the theory that they are only failures because they are victims. And such Great Conspiracy Theories, in all their forms, are shockingly simple to promulgate. Conspiracy-theorizing allows Scavengers to avoid all serious discussions, to dismiss all calls for evidence as themselves evidence of malice. It allows the Scavengers to disregard reality, and to label any system that ends with their failure as one controlled in secretive fashion by a cabal of enemies. Conspiracy-theorizing acts as both sword and shield: an attack on lions, and a shield against their response.

None of this is to argue that there are no rigged systems, no conspiracies. Of course there are. But bold claims about the power of such systems must be matched by compelling evidence. One easy way to tell conspiracy theorists from rational thinkers is how they treat absence of evidence: For the rational thinker, absence of evidence for a theory undermines the theory; for the conspiracy theorist, absence of evidence for a theory may well be evidence that a conspiracy is true. For the conspiracy theorist, the Great Conspiracy Theory is unfalsifiable. And whoever presents an unfalsifiable theory about a Great Conspiracy is, definitionally, acting outside the realm of the rational—and instead acting with corrupt and base motivation.

The Third Principle: Violence Against Others Is the Justified Corrective to Failure

The philosophy of the Scavenger says that your grievances are justified. You are the center around which the rest of the universe turns. If you suffer, you suffer unjustly. And if you suffer unjustly, that must be the result of systems designed purposefully by a cadre of others.

But complaining about the Great Conspiracy Theory often isn't enough to drive change.

Change requires power. And Scavengers attain power, all too often, through violence.

The only way to fight the Great Conspiracy against you, say the Scavengers, is to seize power. Once you have power, you can destroy the Conspiracy and free yourself and those who fight alongside you. You can use your power to eviscerate your enemies, lay them prostrate before you. You can liberate yourself from the chains of failure.

Now you will be a king. A master of your fate, a forger of the world, a giant among your fellow men.

All you require is power.

Power.

Early on the morning of December 4, 2024, Brian Thompson, the CEO of UnitedHealthcare, the nation's largest health insurance company, was shot to death on West Fifty-Fourth Street in New York City, on his way to an investor meeting. The CCTV footage showed a young man wearing a hoodie and backpack approaching Thompson from behind and shooting him three times.

Thompson grew up in Jewell, Iowa, a small, working-class town. His parents weren't wealthy; his mother worked as a beautician and his father at a grain storage facility. Brian did manual labor as a child, graduated from public school, went to the University of Iowa, and joined UnitedHealth Group as a low-level employee twenty years before becoming CEO.[20]

The suspect, it turned out, was a twenty-six-year-old University of Pennsylvania graduate named Luigi Mangione. Mangione grew up in a wealthy family—his family had made its money in nursing homes and owned a country club; he attended a $38,000-per-year Maryland preparatory academy; he earned both undergraduate and graduate degrees from University of Pennsylvania; he got a job at a tech company. While he suffered from severe back pain due to either a childhood condition or a surfing injury or both, the evidence tends to show that he had a successful surgery to alleviate that pain. He was not insured by United HealthCare.

Whatever his mental state, his alleged motivation was made clear in a note found on him when he was arrested:

Frankly, these parasites simply had it coming.... A reminder: the US has the #1 most expensive healthcare system in the world, yet we rank roughly #42 in life expectancy. United is the [indecipherable] largest company in the US by market cap, behind only Apple, Google, Walmart. It has grown and grown, but [h]as our life expectancy? No the reality is, these [indecipherable] have simply gotten too powerful, and they continue to abuse our country for immense profit because the American public has allowed them to get away with it. Obviously the problem is more complex, but I do not have space, and frankly I do not pretend to be the most qualified person to lay out the full argument.... It is not an issue of awareness at this point, but clearly power games at play. Evidently I am the first to face it with such brutal honesty.

This is a nearly Platonic example of the Scavenger philosophy at play.

Mangione was, for whatever reason, seemingly a failure in life. He seems to have failed despite every opportunity—familial, educational, economic. Yet his failure was, allegedly, according to him, the result of a system that required correction. Never mind, he admitted, that the problem is "complex" and that he had no understanding or qualification to argue about solutions. The problem could be reduced, in the end, to "power games at play."

The philosophy of the Scavengers is seductive, all the way from the Garden of Eden to the streets of New York City. So it was little wonder that public support for the accused murderer poured forth. Famed technology and social media journalist Taylor Lorenz, formerly of the *Washington Post*, expressed her "joy" at the shooting. And it wasn't just Lorenz. "Today," wrote one professor at Columbia University, "we mourn the death of United Healthcare CEO Brian Thompson, gunned down ... wait, I'm sorry—today we mourn the deaths of the 68,000

Americans who needlessly die each year so that insurance company execs like Brian Thompson can become multimillionaires." Comedian Bill Burr ranted, "You know, I gotta be honest with you, OK? I love that f***ing CEOs are f***ing afraid right now. You should be! By and large, you're all a bunch of selfish greedy f***ing pieces of s***." Jimmy Kimmel joked on his nighttime program that his producers found the accused shooter attractive.

And why not?

Mangione was allegedly a victim of the system.

And when it turned out he actually wasn't, well, others were.

The health care system was not the outgrowth of a thousand mistakes made at a thousand levels over the course of decades. It was, as Mangione said, a conspiracy of power directed at harming the American people. In the words of Representative Alexandria Ocasio-Cortez, a societal leech par excellence, "I think for anyone who is confused or shocked or appalled, they need to understand that people interpret and feel and experience denied claims as an act of violence against them." Senator Bernie Sanders, a putrescent Marxist pimple on the posterior of the body politic, describes the health care system as a conspiracy: "if you have a system that is designed to make tens of billions a year in profits for insurance companies and drug companies, by definition it is not going to address the needs of the American people."[21]

This, of course, is conspiratorial thinking. And it breeds violence. As Popper explains:

> I do not wish to imply that conspiracies never happen. On the contrary, they are typical social phenomena. They become important, for example, whenever people who believe in the conspiracy theory get into power. And people who sincerely

believe that they know how to make heaven on earth are most likely to adopt the conspiracy theory, and to get involved in a counter-conspiracy against non-existing conspirators. For the only explanation of their failure to produce their heaven is the evil intention of the Devil, who has a vested interest in hell.[22]

The philosophy of the Scavenger is a variety of phantom conspiracies: the racialist conspiracy theory of a dominant white supremacist superstructure in the United States; the Marxist conspiracy theory of an economic elite seeking to rig the economy to the detriment of the working class; the transgressive conspiracy theory of a heteronormative society using its power to fascistically enforce traditional sexual mores; the international conspiracy theory of a settler-colonialist West using its power to promote its ethnocentric ideology. And each conspiracy theory carries with it the implicit promise of violent opposition, deemed morally praiseworthy by the conspiracists.

On October 7, 2024, I visited the grave of Rabbi Menachem Mendel Schneerson, the leader of the Chabad Lubavitch movement, with President Trump. The president's team had asked me to attend the event; I asked if I could bring along with me the family of Edan Alexander, an American-Israeli dual citizen taken hostage by Hamas during the massacre. I had the honor of introducing President Trump to Adi and Yael, Edan's parents, as well as his younger brother, Roy.

"Mr. President," said Yael, "we just want him to come home. He is an amazing boy, and he's an American, and he deserves to come home."

President Trump nodded, and vowed to do all he could to bring him home.

It was a year filled with such tragedy.

I met with widows who lost their husbands on October 7th as they rushed to fight Hamas; widows who lost their husbands while fighting against the terrorist group Hezbollah; children who lost their parents, parents their children.

And I saw those who celebrated their murderers.

I saw them occupying lawns on college campuses, screaming their hatred for Western civilization. I saw them waving trans flags next to Hamas flags. I saw the politicians who support them and the corporations that cave to them and the members of the media who cheer them.

We have all seen them, this motley agglomeration of what Frantz Fanon once called "the wretched of the earth."

They are marching.

In 1922, T. S. Eliot wrote about a world he feared had died in the fires of World War I, in his frightening poem *The Waste Land*:

> *What is that sound high in the air*
> *Murmur of maternal lamentation*
> *Who are those hooded hordes swarming*
> *Over endless plains, stumbling in cracked earth*
> *Ringed by the flat horizon only*
> *What is the city over the mountains*
> *Cracks and reforms and bursts in the violet air*
> *Falling towers*
> *Jerusalem Athens Alexandria*
> *Vienna London*
> *Unreal*[23]

The Scavengers, Eliot wrote, roamed the desolate landscape, picking at the ruins of the civilization they had helped to topple.

Those Scavengers would rise soon enough, damning the world to the worst war in its history.

Civilization survived that war—World War II.

And for a time, the Scavengers hid.

They nursed their hatred.

And they waited.

Now, the Scavengers have returned.

And they are within our walls.

CHAPTER FIVE

THE PACK

LOS ANGELES

I write this from Los Angeles.

We try to visit Los Angeles as little as possible these days.

It wasn't always like this.

I grew up in LA; I spent virtually my entire life here.

I was born in Burbank, California, a firmly middle-class suburb—clean, well run, and friendly—in an 1,100-square-feet home with two bedrooms and a bathroom for six people. As my parents become more observant in their Jewish practice, they sought an Orthodox community, and we moved to Valley Village, where we ended up on a quiet street in a 2,400-square-feet home. That's where I spent the rest of my childhood. At the age of sixteen, I went to college at the University of California, Los Angeles, in Westwood—a shiny college town with a beautiful, sprawling campus at its heart.

When I came back from Harvard Law School, my sister fixed me up with my wife, then a junior at UCLA; she went on to graduate from UCLA Medical School. We bought a condo, then a home, then another home in Valley Village, near my parents, perhaps a mile from where I'd grown up. In 2016 we bought a gorgeous historically preserved Hollywood home—the house where Judy Garland had celebrated her sixteenth-birthday party—and made renovations.

This was supposed to be our forever home.

But things began collapsing.

They began collapsing because Los Angeles—and California more broadly—had spent two decades actively driving away Lions and lionizing Scavengers.

Confiscatory tax rates designed to punish business; public policy that treated homelessness as a right rather than as a plight; a brutal crackdown on the police's ability to fight crime and public disorder; failing public schools combined with a rich set of unfunded welfare benefits; decaying public services.

All of it became more evident in our daily lives.

Whether it was walking past drug addicts passed out face down in the gutter just outside the gates of our home or spotting open needles on the streets where we walked our children, the quality of life in Los Angeles declined slowly . . . and then rapidly . . . and then all at once.

We had considered leaving California in 2018; we decided against it, given how much family we had living in Los Angeles.

But 2020 changed everything.

When the pandemic broke out, the state of California lost its mind. Los Angeles barely had a mind left to lose. Everyone was confined to quarters for months on end.

Schools were closed, despite virtually no data suggesting that Covid was a widespread danger to children.

Public parks were closed, despite a complete absence of data suggesting that Covid could be transferred in open spaces.

Even turnouts on Mulholland Drive were closed, presumably to prevent the possibility of Covid orgies on the side of the road.

Los Angeles began to look like a ghost town.

Then, increasingly, like a zombie apocalypse: The only people allowed to congregate on the streets were the drug-addled and the mentally ill.

But that was just the beginning.

In the aftermath of the death of George Floyd that summer, Los Angeles burst into riots. While the authorities threatened law-abiding citizens for congregating in private or public, Black Lives Matter rioters were allowed to run roughshod over the city. Protesters quickly showed up at the home of Mayor Eric Garcetti—and Garcetti took to the microphones to lecture Angelenos about the evils of systemic racism. Police officers were villainized; they were told to stand down as the city burned. Videos of police cars burning on Melrose Avenue became ubiquitous. Looters smashed the windows of our local Walgreens and Foot Locker. At night, after we put our kids to bed, we could sit in our living room and hear the sounds of helicopters and gunfire nearby. The windows to our business, *The Daily Wire*, had to be boarded up after they were smashed by rioters—rioters our politicians said were merely social justice activists seeking systemic change.

That's when my family decided to leave for Florida.

My company, *The Daily Wire*, packed up and left for Nashville, Tennessee, along with nearly one hundred employees.

Now, four years later, we're back for a family event.

Earlier this evening, we went out to dinner with family friends, a husband and wife from our old neighborhood. The restaurant was in a decent part of the city—not a particularly high-crime area. At dinner, our friends regaled us with the stories of the last several years: being accosted by a knife-wielding mentally ill homeless man in downtown Los Angeles; being victimized in an attempted carjacking.

After the meal, we parted ways in front of the restaurant. My wife and I have 24/7 security; we walked toward our car, which was parked a half block away.

As we got into our car, my wife's phone rang.

It was the wife, sobbing.

She and her husband had just been robbed.

When they had reached their car, another car—a white coupe—screeched to a halt in front of them. Three suspects—all young, black males—had jumped out of the car, grabbed the husband, and yanked him out of the car, stole his watch, phone, and keys, and then rushed around the other side of the car to assault the wife and steal her jewelry. (The physical description of the suspects is relevant here, since they remain at large.)

My security sped down the street to help, but the suspects had fled by the time they arrived. It took the police fifteen minutes to get there. When they did, they were of no help.

Why would they be? In Los Angeles, enforcing the law may land you in jail.

One of my best friends in Los Angeles is a longtime LAPD officer. He, like virtually all the other street cops in the city, applied for a desk job during the BLM riots, knowing that he could spend the rest of his life in jail for simply doing his job. This isn't a rare phenomenon: It's what crime scholar Heather Mac Donald has termed the Ferguson Effect, named after the spike in crime subsequent to the death of black teenager Michael Brown in Ferguson, Missouri. After Brown was justifiably shot—he'd grabbed the gun of a police officer and then charged the police officer when ordered to surrender—the police officer was fully investigated. Police officers across the country took note and began declining to aggressively work the streets. The result: a massive spike in crime.

That is the pattern: Those who seek to destroy society all too often succeed.

They cobble together coalitions of the supposedly oppressed.

They rise up.

And when they seize control, everyone suffers, Scavenger and Lion alike.

The Scavengers, as we have seen, are motivated by envy, by *ressentiment*.

They resonate to the words of the villain Aaron in Shakespeare's *Titus Andronicus*:

If there be devils, would I were a devil,
To live and burn in everlasting fire,
So I might have your company in hell,
But to torment you with my bitter tongue!

The Scavengers do not wish for a better world, or at least a better world for *everyone*; they would rather everyone be equal in misery than that everyone be unequal in prosperity. They would rather live in Hell than in Heaven with their enemies. All that matters is that their enemies are brought low—even if it means that they too are brought low.

The Scavengers have little in common. In fact, it is only their opposition to the West that can explain the odd conglomeration of Scavengers who share a movement. Islamists share a movement with transgender activists; Marxist environmentalists share a movement with Left-wing billionaires. On a logical level, none of this holds together—all these movements are in constant, roiling conflict with one another. Queers for Palestine may constitute a group of scavengers in the West, but in the Middle East, they would be tossed from four-story buildings. But they *can* stick together if their only goal is fighting the Lions.

This phenomenon has been termed the Omnicause by writer Alysia Ames. *The New York Times* sums up the mosaic nature of the enterprise: "In many students' eyes, the war in Gaza is linked to other issues, such as policing, mistreatment of Indigenous people, racism and the impact of climate change."[1]

We hear their screams of rage, their self-righteous chants; we see their banners held aloft. We see them, millions strong.

These are the Looters.

These are the Lechers.

These are Barbarians.

THE LOOTERS

If Lions are hunters—innovators and adventurers, those who seek new answers and break new ground—Scavengers are Looters.

They build nothing of their own.

They simply claim the innovation of others as theirs.

They prowl the earth, seeking to dispossess or even kill those who have more than they.

Karl Marx famously claimed that the history of the world is class struggle: the rich against the poor. "Freeman and slave, patrician and plebeian, lord and serf, guild-master and journeyman, in a word, oppressor and oppressed, stood in constant opposition to one another," he wrote, "carried on an uninterrupted, now hidden, now open fight, a fight that each time ended either in a revolutionary reconstitution of society at large, or in the common ruin of the contending classes."

What sort of revolutionary reconstitution could bridge the gap between the oppressor and oppressed? Only looting: stealing or seizing the essential parts of a system while simultaneously destroying it. The more important the system, the more important that it be emptied, then eviscerated.

Capitalism.

Church.

The family unit.

It all had to be destroyed, in the name of tearing down *unjust systems*.

Marx's thinking checks all the boxes of the Scavenger philosophy: the belief that all systems are merely a guise for exploitative power; that a Great Conspiracy deprives men of their rightful place in the world; and that revolt is the proper and inevitable response.

According to Marx, free markets aren't truly free—they are in fact just another form of slavery. Marx contends that innovators provide nothing; investors provide nothing. Only labor matters. As we have discussed, Marx was a devotee of the faulty labor theory of value, which holds that we can objectively determine the value of a good, product, or service by reference to the labor that went into making it. Capitalists, said Marx, were merely expropriators of the "surplus value" generated by labor. They were, by nature, vampiric bloodsuckers. According to Marx, because capitalists were determined to increase profit, they would therefore have to drive down wages, leading to the relative immiseration of the proletariat. As Marx wrote:

> [W]ithin the capitalist system all methods for raising the social productiveness of labour are brought about at the cost of the individual labourer; all means for the development of production transform themselves into means of domination over, and exploitation of, the producers; they mutilate the labourer into a fragment of a man, degrade him to the level of an appendage of a machine, destroy every remnant of charm in his work and turn it into a hated toil. . . .

Capitalism, Marx said, is a form of slavery that differs from slavery "only in the mode in which this surplus labor is in each case extracted from the actual producer."[2] Investors and innovators are actually bloodsuckers—they steal the "surplus value" from laborers.

Eventually, Marx claimed, there would be revolution. Capitalism would plant the seeds of its own destruction: Eventually, capitalism would lead to a monopolistic class with too much power, and the proletariat would rebel. Marx posited the inevitability of a democratic revolution from below, but he certainly left no doubt about the fate of those who stood in the way of progress: Marx and Engels contended in *The Communist Manifesto* that the bourgeois, the "middle class owner of property," had to be "swept out of the way, and made impossible." Religion, too, had to be destroyed in the name of Marx's pursuit of a utopian vision. So did the nuclear family.[3]

Marx posited his theories as scientific rules of history.

And he was utterly and completely wrong.

Marx's theories predicted an international class revolution; they predicted that well-developed capitalist societies would lead the way into the communist future; they predicted mass immiseration of the working class.

None of this happened.

But his ideological heirs had no such pretensions toward prophecy.

To them, Marx's theories weren't simply specious constructs that had failed in the real world. They were spurs to action. They were righteous calls to violence.

Vladimir Lenin, the most powerful and successful of Marx's heirs, simply reversed the order of action: If Marx had sought a democratic revolution from below, Lenin justified a tyrannical revolution from above—supposedly as a precursor to democratic reform. Lenin stated: "[W]e demand the overthrow of capitalism, the expropriation of the bourgeoisie, as a necessary basis both for the abolition of the poverty of the masses and for the complete and all-round institution of all democratic reforms."[4]

In short, violent revolution first; democracy to be discussed after utopia achieved.

And utopia would be achieved through mass murder.

As Lenin explained:

Is it good that the people should apply such unlawful, irregular, unmethodical and unsystematic methods of struggle as seizing their liberty and creating a new, formally unrecognised and revolutionary authority, that it should use force against the oppressors of the people? Yes, it is very good. It is the supreme manifestation of the people's struggle for liberty.[5]

Lenin was not shy about implementing his dictatorship. In 1918 he sent the following order to his secret police, the Cheka, calling for the mass murder of kulaks—landowners, many of whom were certainly not rich:

> Comrades! The insurrection of five kulak districts should be *pitilessly* suppressed. The interests of the *whole* revolution require this because "the last decisive battle" with the kulaks is now underway *everywhere*. An example must be demonstrated.
>
> 1. Hang (and make sure that the hanging takes places *in full view of the people*) *no fewer than one hundred* known kulaks, rich men, bloodsuckers.
> 2. Publish their names.
> 3. Seize *all* their grain from them.
> 4. Designate hostages in accordance with yesterday's telegram.
>
> Do it in such a fashion that for hundreds of kilometers around the people might see, tremble, know, shout: *they are strangling and will strangle to death the bloodsucking kulaks.*
>
> Telegraph receipt and *implementation*.
> Yours, Lenin.
>
> Find some truly hard people.[6]

Lenin's followers were enthusiastic in their response. Grigory Zinoviev, an original member of the Politburo who would later meet his end at the hands of Stalin, explained, "We must carry along with us 90 million out of the 100 million of Soviet Russia's inhabitants. As for the rest, we have nothing to say to them. They must be annihilated."[7]

Stalin, of course, made Lenin seem mild in his own enthusiasm for vicious brutality: Between deliberately starving millions of his own citizens in Ukraine during the Holodomor—children were found eating the bodies of their siblings, parents the bodies of their children—and purging all he perceived as threats to his rule, Stalin was responsible for somewhere between 6 and 9 million deaths. From activating his minions to wipe out Ukrainian farmers and their families while shouting, "We will make soap of kulaks," to murdering all of his enemies during the Great Purge, Stalin's viciousness knew no bounds. In 1952, the Soviet central committee launched the "Doctors' Plot," accusing Jewish doctors of seeking to kill Stalin. Stalin himself stated, "Every Jew is a nationalist and an agent of American intelligence." Only his death likely prevented more mass killing of Jews.[8]

The Looters are not restricted to the Soviet Union, Cuba, Venezuela, or North Korea.

The Looters exist in nearly every Western society.

They see in their own failure the work of a conspiratorial minority. They see free markets as an artificial creation of the powerful, designed to victimize the powerless. They believe that private property is not a natural right, the result of man's control over his own abilities, but a repossession of the "commons" by the exploitative Lions: those who declare ownership over such property. Jean-Jacques Rousseau, intellectual cornerstone of the French Revolution, and by extension, the Russian Revolution, wrote:

> The first man who, having enclosed a piece of ground, bethought himself of saying This is mine, and found people

simple enough to believe him, was the real founder of civil society. From how many crimes, wars and murders, from how many horrors and misfortunes might not any one have saved mankind, by pulling up the stakes, or filling up the ditch, and crying to his fellows, "Beware of listening to this impostor; you are undone if you once forget that the fruits of the earth belong to us all, and the earth itself to nobody."[9]

Today, communist philosopher Slavoj Zizek idiotically claims, "These ultra-rich corporations are owned by individuals. How did Bill Gates become so rich? He monopolized our commons. If we want to communicate, we have to go through his products. So, it's not profit in the sense of exploiting his workers. It's rent. We are paying him rent, we are paying Jeff Bezos rent, and so on, and so on."[10]

But of course, there is no "commons" that includes the technological development created by innovators within free markets. Bill Gates no more "monopolized our commons" than Steve Jobs monopolized the iPhone. Private property is the basis of liberty and prosperity; the Looters despise both. What they wish for, instead, is *control*—and that desire for control can justify even terror and ruin. There is a reason Zizek winkingly endorses the French Revolution's murderous Reign of Terror under Robespierre.[11]

The end of societies run by the Looters is ruin—as it must be.

A parasite without a host is doomed to die.

Ayn Rand describes the process well in *Atlas Shrugged*:

Such looters believe it safe to rob defenseless men, once they've passed a law to disarm them. But their loot becomes the magnet for other looters, who get it from them as they got it. Then the race goes, not to the ablest at production, but to those most ruthless at brutality. When force is the standard, the murderer wins over the pickpocket. And then that society vanishes, in a spread of ruins and slaughter.[12]

THE LECHERS

The Roman Emperor Nero (AD 37–68) holds a particularly seedy place in the popular imagination. A bisexual reprobate of heroic order, Nero held wild sexual orgies in the streets of Rome, engaged in the rape and murder of men and women, and set Christians alight. According to the historian Tacitus, "Nero, who polluted himself by every lawful or lawless indulgence, had not omitted a single abomination which could heighten his depravity...."[13]

Nero's moral corruption was so famously excessive that he has in many ways become synonymous with libertine sin.

But there's another side to Nero that must be understood: Nero the politician.

Nero's penchant for social leveling—according to Tacitus, his orgies featured "brothels crowded with noble ladies, and on the opposite bank were seen naked prostitutes"—made him popular with the lower classes. He clearly sought to wipe away the more traditional moral universe of Augustus Caesar and his heirs in pursuit of public approval. At his death, Tacitus writes, he was mourned by "[t]he degraded populace, frequenters of the arena and the theatre, the most worthless of the slaves, and those who having wasted their property were supported by the infamous excesses of Nero...."[14]

It turns out that one road to power for the Scavenger is the road of excess—the road of Lechery.

For much of human history, people have chafed at the restrictions of sexual morality. Human beings have a tendency to identify with their desires—to believe that they *are* merely a compendium of their desires. This is nothing new; it is as old as time. It is precisely this that Paul warned against in his First Epistle to the Corinthians:

> Flee from sexual immorality. Every other sin a person commits is outside the body, but the sexually immoral person sins against his own body. Or do you not know that your body is a temple of the Holy Spirit within you, whom you have from God? You are not your own, for you were bought with a price. So glorify God in your body.[15]

Traditional morality sees the locus of individual identity as a symbiotic relationship between the atomistic individual and society. We are born with certain biological characteristics, which restrict our choices in life but also grant us certain abilities; we are born into a preexisting social system, with roles and responsibilities.

We are both individual and communal beings.

We adapt our individual characteristics to the civilization around us. As philosopher Carl Trueman writes:

> It is in communal activities that individuals find their true selves; the true self in traditional cultures is therefore something that is given and learned, not something that the individual creates for himself. . . .[16]

The Lecher sees the core of individual identity in his unfettered desires.

In short: We are what we want.

Societal forces that cut against the feeling, that refuse to celebrate that feeling, are oppressive and ought to be shattered.

Those forces are a Great Conspiracy against our happiness, and must be destroyed. Again, as Trueman explains:

> The intuitive moral structure of our modern social imaginary prioritizes victimhood, sees selfhood in psychological terms, regards traditional sexual codes as oppressive and life denying, and places a premium on the individual's right to define his or her own existence....[17]

And as Trueman rightly points out, any rejection of the individual's self-definition is treated as a "moral offense" to be punished.

The Lecher believes that true happiness is to be found in the evisceration of all rules, roles, and obligations. But the morality of the Lecher isn't a call to a higher human life; it's actually a call to return to the animal. It requires that any inhibiting institutions be obliterated in order to free man to rut as he pleases. The Marquis de Sade, whose very name would become the embodiment of Lechery (*sadism* comes from the name Sade), boasts just as much:

> I was still very young when I learned to hold religion's fantasies in contempt, being perfectly convinced that the existence of a creator is a revolting absurdity in which not even children continue to believe. I have no need to thwart my inclinations

in order to flatter some god; these instincts were given me by Nature, and it would be to irritate her were I to resist them; if she gave me bad ones, that is because they were necessary to her designs. I am in her hands but a machine which she runs as she likes, and not one of my crimes does not serve her: the more she urges me to commit them, the more of them she needs; I should be a fool to disobey her.[18]

This supposed freedom doesn't result in fulfillment, of course. Instead, Lechery results in deep unhappiness.

We are far more than our genitals. We are *embedded beings*—embedded in our time, embedded in our society, embedded in our family. Removing from us all of those connections leaves us aimless, confused. What's more, linking our sexual desires with our identities dispenses with other aspects of individuality that have typically characterized human beings: our freedom of action, our reason, our sympathies. Reducing human beings to a Freudian sex impulse flattens them entirely.

Lechery commits the failing of treating both *behavior* and *desire* as immutable characteristics, akin to race or sex, thus removing from us freedom and responsibility—which, presumably, is a feature rather than a bug.

But behavior *can* be trained, controlled, shaped by environment.

Indeed, it must be.

That is the essence of the *Lion's* philosophy—that we are made in the image of God.

The Lecher, as a Scavenger, insists that we are merely beasts, and in fact ought to be.

In fact, the Lecher insists that we teach our children the ways of Lechery—as early as possible, in all their perversion.

For the Lechers, Western tradition and culture is the enemy. And Western tradition and culture must be removed from society by any means necessary, as early as possible.

The political Left has been extraordinarily successful in this pursuit. Marriage rates have declined to all-time lows; so have birth rates. Even as all limits on Lechery have disappeared, both male and female happiness have declined (women far more than men, on a relative scale).[19] The sexual revolution—the revolution of the Lechers—has indeed overthrown the existing order, destroying millions of lives in the process.

The Lechers are not restricted to the radical Left.

A reactionary "manosphere" Conspiracy Theory has emerged on the Right to match the transgressive Lechery of the Left.

In this reactionary view, traditional morality is also the enemy—because traditional morality has failed to defeat the Lechers. Thus traditional morality must be discarded, and we must return to a time *before* such morality. The best possible system is one in which men engage in physical aggression, emotionless promiscuity, avoidance of commitment. Be a lone wolf.

That's the message of online influencers like Andrew Tate. Tate, of course, is best known as a WWE-type macho man, strutting around his rather ugly Romanian mansion, taking pictures next to expensive sports cars, and jabbering about escaping "The Matrix"—which he can help *you* do too, if you join Hustlers University, for the low, low price of $49.99 per month to start (the prices elevate quickly to the thousands of dollars). Tate boasts tens of millions of followers on social media; in 2023, he was the third-most-googled person on the planet.[20]

According to Tate, he is a victim of the Matrix, and so are you. The Matrix, of course, is a gormless "gynocracy" that seeks to rob men of their virility and power. The only way to regain that virility and power is to dominate other men and women using intimidation, threat, or force. As Tate says, "Life is war. It's a war for the female you want. It's a war for the money you want. It's a war for the status. Masculine life is war!" Tate has never served in the military, of course. Tate, not coincidentally, is currently facing multiple charges in Romania, including sex trafficking, rape, and forming an organized criminal group. Nonetheless, he was greeted as a hero by many in the United States when he visited in March 2025.

To Tate, women are burdens or idiots, to be either abused, exploited, or avoided. Tate pretends at masculinity while pimping out women for money as cam girls: Tate has bragged, "There's no such thing as having girls who work for you who you've not f***ed. It's impossible. You have to f*** them, and they have to love you. It's essential to the business, because otherwise women have no loyalty." When challenged, Tate flexes his biceps while smoking a cigar, and dares anyone to call him unmanly. A former kickboxing champion, he seems to believe that because he was good at kicking other men in the face, he can now unshoulder the burden of actual manliness—the obligations that come along with being a man.

Obligations like, say, treating women decently, or forming a traditional family.

Now, an enormous amount of talk from the so-called manosphere is simply trollish dumbassery. When Tate theorizes about hitting women, that's just imbecilic posturing by a nasty jester (there are multiple ongoing accusations—all of which he denies—that Tate does more than theorize about such activities). But unfortunately, this "red pill" theory of masculinity has gone viral. It is the mood of the moment.

That's because unlike the feminist movement's catastrophic and thoroughly false deconstruction of manhood, there is a grain of truth to the Conspiracy Theory promoted by Tate: The sexual revolution did indeed rob men of their historic roles as hunters, warriors, and weavers. The Lion's solution would be for men to reembrace their roles *as Lions*: to reclaim their masculinity by becoming providers, protectors, and community-builders. Tate's proposed solution, by contrast—to embrace a life of Lechery and perversity—is no solution at all. In fact, it's the mirror image of what Left-wing Lechers propose.

Lechers make odd bedfellows.

THE BARBARIANS

Not all cultures are morally equivalent.

It's a lesson the West refuses to learn.

The year is 1946, and Zahir Shah, king of Afghanistan, has decided to build his nation. Americans, sponsored by the United States government, soon descend on the war-torn nation to participate. As Rajiv Chandrasekaran writes, they proceed to spend millions of dollars building dams, irrigation networks, and even American-style villages complete with "white-stucco homes, green front lawns ... and a co-ed high school where boys and girls frolicked together." Afghans took to calling that village "Little America."

In Little America, American-style habits were encouraged: education for girls, for example. Historian Arnold Toynbee gushed, "American-mindedness is the characteristic mark of the whole band of Afghan technicians and administrators who are imposing Man's will on the Helmand River." Afghanistan, it seemed, might actually enter an upward spiral of development.

It would all go to waste.

The soil upon which the Americans planted was too shallow—but even worse, local Afghans refused to stop flooding the fields, destroying the minerals in the soil. The locals refused to build ditches for drainage. By 1959 it was clear that many Afghans would resist civilization. Riots broke out after the government tried to abolish the forced veiling of women, targeting a girls' school in Kandahar. As Chandrasekaran says, by 1960 the Americans had abandoned their quest at cultural change, focusing instead on the merely economic.

Even that wasn't enough.

In order to make the Helmand River Valley a productive agricultural center, the Americans would have had to temporarily remove farmers and bulldoze their land to stop the drainage. Farmers grabbed their rifles and threatened the workers. With the agricultural centers reduced to subsistence levels, the Afghan government had no revenue to build infrastructure that might have made the country more productive.

The Soviet invasion of 1979 ended Little America once and for all.

Afghans still use much of the irrigation system created by the Americans and their Afghan allies decades ago; the American-built Kajaki Dam still works to an extent. But those tens of millions of dollars were wasted.[21] Yes, much of that can be chalked up to American blundering. But more can be chalked up to the mentality of the Afghans who refused to participate in their own betterment, and saw the West's help as merely a form of soft conquest.

In Rudyard Kipling's poem "The Pict," he describes the mindset well:

We shall be slaves just the same?
Yes, we have always been slaves.
But you—you will die of shame,
And then we shall dance on your graves.[22]

The patron saint of such thought in the modern era is Frantz Fanon. Fanon believed that the West was a colonizing power—and that natives had the moral duty to destroy that power, no matter what came next. Better for the barbarians to win, even if that meant a descent into barbarism. An ardent member of the Algerian National Liberation Front, Fanon put forth a shockingly violent treatise calling for the revolution of the colonized against their colonizers in his 1961 book, *The Wretched of the Earth*. Fanon didn't merely call for the end of colonialism, à la Gandhi. Instead he called for violence, which he saw as purifying, in all its varied forms. Fanon theorized that revolutionary violence would usher in the New Man, free of the evils of the West.

"In its bare reality," Fanon wrote, "decolonization reeks of red-hot cannonballs and bloody knives."

Violence. Disorder. Bloody knives.

What would be the purpose of such decolonization?

What would come next?

Fanon didn't know, and he didn't care.

The decolonization itself *was* the point. Decolonization would create "new men." As he wrote:

> [D]ecolonization is always a violent phenomenon.... [D]ecolonization is quite simply the replacing of a certain "species" of men by another "species" of men. Without any period of transition, there is a total, complete, and absolute

substitution.... Decolonization, which sets out to change the order of the world, is, obviously, a program of complete disorder.[23]

This was all part of Fanon's own Great Conspiracy Theory.

That theory suggests that all failings of a colonized people are the result of the colonizers. Capitalism's focus on good relations, moral order, and harmonious relations is merely a guise for exploitation; the exploited are therefore justified in their hatred. "The look that the native turns on the settler's town is a look of lust, a look of envy," argued Fanon. "[I]t expresses his dreams of possession—all manner of possession: to sit at the settler's table, to sleep in the settler's bed, with his wife if possible. The colonized man is an envious man... there is no native who does not dream at least once a day of setting himself up in the settler's place."[24]

And this envy is good and justified, per Fanon. For lurking in the Scavenger's heart is a new man, a lion unchained: "For the native, life can spring up again out of the rotting corpse of the settler."[25] While Looters seek to steal that which is valuable from a system, then tear down the system and build something new, Barbarians are content with destruction alone. That destruction, they believe, leads to their own spiritual renaissance.

That is the essence of Fanon's decolonization. The colonized must destroy everything in the name of restoring himself as a human being.

Decolonization justifies any response. In fact, it *requires* any response. The West must be destroyed, for the West has colonized. "When the colonized hear a speech on Western culture they draw their machetes or at least check to see they are close at hand," Fanon says. "In the colonial context the settler only ends his work of breaking in the native when the latter admits loudly and intelligibly the supremacy of the white man's values. In the period of decolonization, the colonized masses mock at these very values, insult them, and vomit them up."[26]

As it turns out, however, many of those values are prerequisites for success. Indeed, Fanon's Algerian revolution would carry with it no dream of a brighter day. In the aftermath of France's recognition of Algerian independence in 1962, chaos, military dictatorship, and radical Islamism followed. Six decades after independence, Algeria remains a dictatorship with minimal economic development outside of its oil industry.

Such hatred of colonial power was at least somewhat understandable in Algeria, which lived with decades of brutal French repression. But Fanon wasn't making the case for revolutionary violence merely there. He was making the case for revolutionary violence *everywhere*.

The man who made *that* clear was existentialist and Marxist Jean-Paul Sartre. Sartre's introduction to Fanon's *Wretched of the Earth* makes the case not only that the colonized have an ultimate right to violence, but that the entire West must be collapsed from within for its great sins. The West, Sartre argues, is fundamentally evil and cruel; colonialism is merely a symptom of the underlying cancer. Sartre agrees with Fanon that the death of the European colonizer is an inherent good: "to shoot down a European is to kill two birds with one stone, to destroy an oppressor and the man he oppresses at the same time: there remain a dead man, and a free man. . . ."[27]

We must recognize, Sartre explains, that we are all complicit in "a thousand-year-old oppression. . . . You know well enough that we are exploiters. . . . Our precious sets of values begin to molt; on closer scrutiny you won't see one that isn't stained with blood."[28]

Thus the only honorable thing for the West to do is to *join in* on its cultural suicide. In fact, says Sartre, poetic justice for the colonizer comes through the destruction of Western civilization from within: "It's our turn to tread the path, step by step, which leads down to native level. But to become natives altogether, our soil must be occupied by a formerly colonized people and we must starve of hunger."[29]

The Barbarians must enter the gates.

And then the children of the West must join the Barbarians.

This has been one of the major ongoing projects at America's finest universities, where department after department has fallen to the Barbarians—those who seek to tear down the West using the tools of the West, all while recruiting the children of the West to their cause.

Take, for example, Edward Said.

Edward Said was a Palestinian Christian who grew up in Cairo, Egypt, in relative wealth (despite his false protestations that he was in fact a refugee from Jerusalem); as a teenager he was sent abroad, to America, for his education.[30] He graduated from Princeton University and received a master's from Harvard. In 1963 he became a faculty member at Columbia University, in English literature. He would go on to teach at a variety of prestigious institutions, from Harvard to Stanford to Yale. By the time of his death, Said's writings would be taught in hundreds of courses across America.

Said was no expert in geopolitics—far from it. But he *did* have a theory—a Conspiracy Theory that would be called *postcolonialism*.

Following in the footsteps of Fanon, Said argues that Western culture ("the Occident") paints a picture of an excluded, different Other ("the Orient"). This picture, he says, is steeped in ethnocentric falsehood. In short, the West creates a false East so as to label it and attack it. Quoting Foucault, Said defines Orientalism "as a Western style for dominating, restructuring, and having authority over the Orient."[31]

Said's Great Conspiracy Theory, like Fanon's and Sartre's, lays blame for the failure of non-Western cultures at the hands of an oppressive West. Said posits that Orientalists constructed a self-serving reality about the evils of the East in order to justify repression—but that supposition rests on the notion that Eastern cultures and Western cultures are morally equivalent to begin with, and that any perceived inequality is a result of ethnocentrism and racism.

That is a lie.

Some cultures *are in fact better than other cultures.* The culture of the Syrian refugees who harass women at German Christmas markets is *inferior* to the culture of a West that bars such harassment. The Afghans of the 1950s weren't American, and some seventy years later, the same holds true. Radical Islam, for example—for which Said generally made excuses, blaming the West for its excesses, just as Fanon did—correlates with low economic and educational development, mistreatment of women, cruelty toward religious minorities, and high levels of violent conflict. Blaming Orientalism for the problem is a way of deliberately shifting blame. It is a way of asserting control. Said was projecting all along: He wanted power, and he sought it by labeling his opponents cultural supremacists.

Said's theory was never about truth—it was about politics.

It is *always* about politics.

Said was a member of the Palestine National Council, the governing body of the terrorist Palestine Liberation Organization. The year after he released *Orientalism*, he released another book—this time an apologia for Palestinian terrorism titled *The Question of Palestine*. Said himself admitted that he wrote *Orientalism* as a way of making a broader argument about the Israeli-Palestinian conflict: "I don't think I would have written that book had I not been politically associated with a struggle. The struggle of Arab and Palestinian nationalism is very important to that book."[32]

Said's goal was to connect all the populations supposedly subjugated by the West. Despite the fact that Jews have a historic connection with the land of Israel that predates any Muslim claims by nearly two millennia, Said's argument was that Israel was a settler-colonial state, just like South Africa.[33] In fact, said Said, the real problem was that the West had engaged in a centuries-long project of colonialism in which Israel was merely a symptom of a culture dedicated to the proposition that "Europeans always ought to rule non-Europeans."[34]

That argument found eager followers among American Leftists.

Take, for example, Ta-Nehisi Coates.

Coates—a devotee of Said—characterizes America as a colonialist power *within America*. This seems self-contradictory—how can America colonize itself? But as it turns out, all people who are not members of a "colonizing" power—the "colonizing" power, in this case, being white people—are the colonized, and thus victims. The American Dream, in Coates's view, is surrender to the settler-colonialist ideology:

> The forgetting is habit, is yet another necessary component of the Dream. They have forgotten the scale of theft that enriched them in slavery; the terror that allowed them, for a century, to pilfer the vote; the segregationist policy that gave them their suburbs.... I am convinced that the Dreamers, at least the Dreamers of today, would rather live white than live free.[35]

Black Americans, says Coates, like Fanon's colonized Algerians, have internalized the evils of their victimizers; their sins are not their own, but the result of their colonization. "The plunder of black life was drilled into this country in its infancy and reinforced across its history, so that plunder has become an heirloom, an intelligence, a sentience, a default setting to which, likely to the end of our days, we must invariably return,"[36] Coates writes in *Between the World and Me*, a book that has sold some 1.5 million copies and routinely finds its way onto college syllabi. Like Said, Coates stands in solidarity with violent terrorists who seek the destruction of the West, since those terrorists are merely oppressed peoples crying out for vengeance: "I remember watching *World News Tonight* with my father, and deriving from him a dull sense that the Israelis were 'white' and the Palestinians were 'Black,' which is to say that the former were the oppressors and the latter the oppressed."[37]

It should also be no shock that the Barbarians have no problem with attacks on Americans or Westerners more generally.

It was Said who justified 9/11 as "an imperial power injured at home for the first time."[38]

It was Coates who said he watched 9/11 impassively: "They were not human to me. Black, white, or whatever, they were menaces of nature; they were the fire, the comet, the storm, which could—with no justification—shatter my body."[39]

And this year, 1,700 sociology professors wrote an open letter justifying Hamas's October 7th atrocities by placing it "in the context of 75 years of settler colonial occupation and European empire."[40]

The Barbarians are here.

They teach at our universities.

They march in our streets.

And they seek our demise.

The Barbarians never posit a moral justification for the destruction of the Western order at their hands. They never explain just how, for example, a Palestinian state is somehow a burgeoning wellspring of human rights, or how an America without American values would make the world a better place.

The only thing that matters is the destruction of the West—for in that destruction lies the supposed reclamation of the Barbarian identity.

A PECULIAR TYPE

Aside from their base envy, how can we describe the Scavengers?

As we have discussed, Lions are creative, determined, and audacious; they are steadfast, prudent, merciful, and strong.

Scavengers are something else entirely.

In his book *The True Believer,* Eric Hoffer explains that those who tear down the societies in which they live are typically what he terms "inferiors":

> [T]he failures, misfits, outcasts, criminals, and all those who have lost their footing, or never had one, in the ranks of respectable humanity.... They see their lives and the present as spoiled beyond remedy, and they are ready to waste and wreck both: hence their recklessness and their will to chaos and anarchy.[41]

Among the Scavengers are emotional types—and many of the Scavengers fulfill more than one type.

First, there are the *vengeful*.

They are those who are angry at the system that they believe has laid them low. The man stricken by poverty who seeks his daily wage is no Scavenger—he is a provider, an impoverished Lion but still a Lion. The man who believes that he was unfairly deprived of success, and who has free time to pursue his vendetta—that man becomes a Scavenger. As Hoffer says, "Those who see their lives as spoiled and wasted crave equality and fraternity more than they do freedom."[42]

Next, there are the *alienated*.

The alienated are often members of a partially assimilated identity group—a sort of insider/outsider. The man who has few ties that bind him to his group, but who identifies his lack of success with a feeling of exclusion from a broader stream of social life—he often becomes a Scavenger. As historian Mary Matossian explains, intellectuals in colonialized countries provide a particularly good example of dissatisfied revolutionary types, uncomfortable as they are in their own "in-between" status:

> The intellectual may resent the West, but since he is already at least partly Westernized, to reject the West completely would be to deny part of himself. . . . He feels that something must be done, and done fast. . . . Often he scorns his kind (and by implication, himself) as "pseudo," "mongrel," neither truly native nor truly Western. . . . The "assaulted" intellectual works hard to make invidious comparisons between his own nation and the West.[43]

It is hard not to hear echoes of Fanon, Said, and Coates here.

Third, there are the *unappreciated*.

These are the pseudo-intellectual and the artistically unsuccessful, who believe their talents are unappreciated by their supposed inferiors. Their talents are generally underwhelming, but they believe their talents to be thanklessly ignored; their expectations run far out of line with reality. In such frustration lies the breeding ground for Scavengers. It is no coincidence that Hitler was a frustrated painter and that Mao saw himself as an intellectual unappreciated by his society.

Finally, there are simply the *bored*.

Scavengers are plentiful among those for whom life is too easy. It is one of the great ironies of history that revolutionaries are typically drawn not from the ranks of the abject poor but from the idle bourgeoisie. The bored are those who need not struggle for their daily bread, who are not dedicated to the demands of family, who are disengaged from the larger community. They seek a feeling of meaning that can be found in either building or tearing down—and finding themselves incapable of building, they choose the latter option. University students are all too often the seedbed for revolution for precisely this reason: They have no families to support, they are often supported by their parents, and they have intellectual pretensions of their own.

The frisson of blood often excites the Scavengers. In the name of pseudo-justice, the Scavenger becomes a hero to the group by expressing his willingness to do violence. This type was common in pre-Soviet Russia, where terrorism became an intellectual pastime. As terrorist murderer Sergei Stepniak wrote in his book celebrating other terrorists, *Underground Russia: Revolutionary Profiles and Sketches from Life*, "Noble, terrible, irresistibly fascinating ... [the terrorist] combines in himself the two sublimities of human grandeur: the martyr and the hero."[44]

The Russian revolutionaries all saw themselves as members of the *intelligentsia*—not, as scholar Gary Saul Morson says, because they were intellectuals, but because they were frustrated, alienated, or bored ideologues: "The people at the top are wealthy businesspeople, and you're an intellectual. You think that people of ideas should be at the top." These terrorists had nothing but "contempt for the working class and a greater contempt for the peasantry."[45] Their overweening arrogance, combined with alienation from mainstream society, ended in terror, as Dostoevsky predicted in *The Possessed*, in which characters muse on the possibility of cutting off a "hundred million heads." Dostoevsky also presciently predicted that these intellectuals would be successful in convincing liberal thinkers to go along with them: "I could make them go through fire," one of his terrorist leaders says. "One has only to din it into them that they are not advanced enough."[46] Between January 1908 and June 1910 in Russia, nearly 20,000 terrorist attacks and robberies were reported, killing almost 3,800 people.[47]

It is no surprise, then, that the Scavengers are all too often drawn from the ranks of the pathological. The Dark Triad personality traits, as characterized by psychologists, often show up among Scavengers: narcissism (obsession with one's own superiority), Machiavellianism (treating people as means rather than ends), and psychopathy (exploitativeness). Such personality traits are highly associated with authoritarianism: According to one study, Dark Triad traits are associated with both white identitarianism and Left-wing authoritarianism:

> Individuals high in authoritarianism—regardless of whether they hold politically correct or right-wing views—tend to score highly on [Dark Triad] and entitlement. Such individuals therefore are statistically more likely than average to be higher in psychopathy, narcissism, Machiavellianism and entitlement.[48]

Again, this is unsurprising. The Great Conspiracy Theory attracts those who seek to manipulate others. And what better tool for manipulation than positing a Great Conspiracy that can only be overthrown if you are granted overweening power and control?

Greek mythology tells the story of Hercules, who was given a series of tasks by the gods. His second was the killing of the many-headed Hydra. The Hydra, according to Greek historian Apollodorus, "had a huge body, with nine heads, eight mortal, but the middle one immortal."

It had yet another frightening quality: For every head Hercules cut off, two grew in its place.

The Hydra has been for centuries an oft-used description of the mob. In Shakespeare's *Coriolanus*, the great general is stopped in his ambitions to become consul by rioters, manipulated by demagogues. He rages:

> *O good but most unwise patricians! why,*
> *You grave but reckless senators, have you thus*
> *Given Hydra here to choose an officer,*
> *That with his peremptory "shall," being but*
> *The horn and noise o' the monster's, wants not spirit*
> *To say he'll turn your current in a ditch,*
> *And make your channel his?*[49]

That Hydra does indeed thwart Coriolanus's ambitions, and brings about the near destruction of Rome.

The Hydra is a scavenger with many heads.

The Scavengers are not all alike. Indeed, they often hate one another nearly as much as they hate their common enemy.

Almost.

Their common enemy brings them together.

We are their common enemy.

And they are gaining on us.

CHAPTER SIX

THE RULES OF THE PACK

AUSCHWITZ, POLAND

The wind cuts my face as we exit the travel vehicles, into a nondescript parking lot off the side of a winding road near Krakow, Poland.

The cameras are there to meet us.

When we get out of the travel vehicles, we all shake hands: me, Elon Musk, a Holocaust survivor named Gidon Lev. Elon has brought along his young son, who rides on his shoulders. The guides move us toward the entrance of the Auschwitz camp, toward the infamous wrought-iron gates that reads ARBEIT MACHT FREI, work sets you free, a slogan originally designed to deceive those who would be murdered that Auschwitz-Birkenau was a labor camp, not a death camp.

This is my first visit to Auschwitz.

I had never felt the need to come to visit the most notorious mass-killing site in human history. I knew Jewish history; though I am a fourth-generation American on both sides of my family, much of my extended family died in the Holocaust. But when Elon's team called me and asked me to attend his visit, I felt it was an opportunity to stand in solidarity with him and against the rising tide of anti-Semitism.

Auschwitz I—the original camp—is itself smaller than you would imagine, covering an area about 1,000 meters long and 400 meters wide. It was originally constructed as a concentration camp for Polish soldiers captured by the Nazi army but was converted into a death camp two years later. Crematoria originally constructed to burn the bodies of those who had died were themselves expanded and converted to be able to burn the bodies of those exterminated. Prisoners were shaved, deloused, and crammed into brick barracks where disease ran rampant.

We are shown rooms filled with human hair shaved from the heads of those who were later murdered; rooms filled with their shoes.

The room that shocks me most was the room filled with suitcases—every suitcase packed by someone who stuffed what they could of their life into it, expecting to begin a new life at the end of the cattle car journey to Auschwitz. Every one of those suitcases represents a person, an individual with dreams and hopes and a history. Now all those people are ashes. All that is left is their suitcases, looted by the Nazis.

Elon is both engaged and contemplative.

I cannot help but be silent throughout the tour, seeing the place where so many of my coreligionists were exterminated.

But Auschwitz I isn't nearly as shocking to me as Auschwitz II–Birkenau.

Auschwitz II–Birkenau is located approximately two miles from Auschwitz I.

It is only here that you can see the mass industrialization of death.

We walk through the horrifyingly innocuous gate of Auschwitz II–Birkenau, where trains passed day and night carrying hundreds of thousands from the far-flung provinces of Nazi-occupied Europe. You can hear it on the wind, through the brutal cold: the echoing voices from eighty years ago of human beings being unloaded from the cattle cars, separated into lines representing life and death, the voices of children calling for their mothers, wives wailing for their husbands.

All that is left now are the seemingly endless frozen fields of barracks—barracks that were crowded with the sick, the unfed, the dying. People forced to sleep five deep on bunks built for two; people forced not to urinate or defecate given lack of toilets. The roofs are separated from the walls of the barracks, so the wind whistles through the icy rooms. We are clad in heavy jackets; they would have been clad in thin prison uniforms.

And these were the lucky ones.

Those in the lines marked for death would have been ushered into the gas chambers.

All that is left of the crematoria now are ruins. The day before its liberation, the Nazis destroyed Crematoria V.

We stand silently looking at the wreckage of a place where hundreds of thousands of people were led to their deaths. Overall, historians estimate around 1.1 million people were murdered by the Nazis in the Auschwitz camp network.

At the end of our visit, Elon, Gidon, and I are offered the opportunity to light candles in honor of the memories of the slain.

The quiet is oppressive.

Later, I have a chance to speak with Elon. He is by nature an optimist—a person who believes the best about human beings. So much of his aspirational attitude, an attitude that has led him to explore the stars, to create the largest electric car company on the planet, to restore free speech to Twitter, is rooted in that optimism. He seems stunned by the experience. He tells me, "It was incredibly moving and deeply sad and tragic that humans could do this to other humans."

How could such a thing happen?

That has been the question that has animated so much of Western thought for decades since the Holocaust. Was the Nazi ideology rooted in the flaws of Europe? In the nature of nationalism? In opposition to communism or Christianity or secularism?

The answer is actually far simpler: Nazism and its murderous barbarism were a reflection of the impulses of the Scavenger, put into practice. Nazism was, above all, a Great Conspiracy Theory: a belief that Germany had been "sold out" by a small cadre of backstabbers during World War I; a perverse notion that true Germanness had been subverted by an alien nation and philosophy within; a hatred for systems of freedom whose results might not accord with the strict racialist hierarchy so beloved by the Nazis, and a recasting of those systems as part of the broader anti-German conspiracy. Hitler, in *Mein Kampf*, contended that the "Bavarian Center" had sold out the German people to the Jews and Marxists; a "new philosophy" had to be promulgated via the mechanisms of absolute power:

> The bourgeois world is Marxist, but believes in the possibility of the rule of certain groups of men (bourgeoisie), while Marxism itself systematically plans to hand the world over to the Jews.... In opposition to this, the folkish philosophy finds the importance of mankind in its basic racial elements.... Human culture and civilization on this continent are inseparably bound up with the presence of the Aryan.... We all sense that in the distant future humanity must be faced by problems which only a highest race, become master people and supported by the

means and possibilities of an entire globe, will be equipped to overcome.[1]

The Scavengers always require a mythology.
A crass and ignoble mythology: the way of the Scavenger.
They then translate that mythology into a set of rules.
The rules are arbitrary, ugly, and contradictory.
They are inherently unstable.
They are *designed* to be so.
The instability is the point. The Pride is by nature built on hierarchy, which means that it requires stability. The Pack stands for anarchy and chaos; it is fundamentally oppositional. Any stable set of positive rules would prevent the Pack from acting as an untrammeled force of opposition: the Pack would be bound by some higher set of morals. The Pack, when in opposition, is anarchic.

The Pack, in victory, is tyrannical. Chaos cannot be allowed to reign—and a set of rules might establish its own hierarchy of winners and losers. Thus the Pack must function as a *permanent revolution*—a Hobbesian tyrant of arbitrary power, eviscerating all enemies in its path. To justify that tyranny, the Pack must constantly orient itself against a common enemy.

That enemy is the Lions.

The Scavengers must reject the rules of the Lion—for the rules of the Lion establish a meritocracy that allows people to succeed or fail as *individuals*. And that is the thing that the Pack can *never* abide. The rules of the pack, therefore, aren't actually rules—they are a *rejection of the rules of the Lion*.

Free minds must be chained.
Free markets must be wrecked.

Public virtue must be undermined.

The rule of law must be destroyed.

RULE #1: THE PACK MUST CONTROL FREE MINDS

Where the Pride revels in free minds, the Pack rejects them.

Free minds are a threat. Free minds might innovate; they might succeed; they might build. Scavengers cannot allow that possibility.

So how can Scavengers justify their tyranny of thought? As always, they invert the truth: They accuse their enemies, advocates of free thought, of being the *true* tyrants. They do so by suggesting that support for freedom of thought is actually a result of *false consciousness*. You don't *actually* like freedom of thought—you've just been indoctrinated to believe you do by a powerful, silent system. You are a victim of the greatest of all Conspiracy Theories: You have lost control of your own mind *already*. You *say* you want freedom of thought, but that's just because the powerful have told you that's what you have—in reality, you have been unconsciously bound up by a system beyond your control. You *never* had freedom of thought in the first place.

In fact, tyranny is the only system that can *set you free*.

This rule of the Pack is a corollary of the Foucauldian supposition that all civilizations and value systems are guises for power. Its first iteration came, unsurprisingly, from Marx and Engels. Marx and Engels wondered just why so few people seemed to think of themselves in terms of class rather than family, nationality, or religion. Their answer was that people had been indoctrinated, their power of class consciousness—*true consciousness* of the need for a class uprising—

removed by the capitalist superstructure. This capitalist false consciousness inexorably led to people thinking as (horror of horrors!) individuals. Marx wrote in 1870 that any antagonisms between people on a basis other than class was the result of manipulation by "the press, the pulpit, the comic papers, in short, by all the means at the disposal of the ruling classes.... It is the secret by which the capitalist class maintains its power. And the latter is quite aware of this."[2] Engels used the phrase "false consciousness" itself in a letter in 1893.[3]

Yet the predicted class revolution never seemed to come. This meant that either Marxism was wrong, or millions of people had been duped.

Naturally, Marxists were not about to admit that they had been wrong.

As Marxism failed in its historic predictions, it became more and more necessary for them to intensify their reliance on the idea of false consciousness.

Lenin, who obviously had the most invested in the success of the Marxist philosophy, recentered false consciousness as a vital component of his worldview. To explain just why Marxism had to be imposed by intellectuals from above in Russia, rather than as a result of Marx's predicted revolution of the working class, Lenin explained that working-class people had been blinded by the systems in which they had been raised. It would require *outsiders*—rebel members of the bourgeoisie themselves—to destroy the ideological foundations of the prevailing capitalist system: "there could not have been Social-Democratic consciousness among the workers. It would have to be brought to them from without."[4]

Simultaneously, Italian socialist Antonio Gramsci posited that false consciousness lay at the root of Marxism's failure to take hold internationally. The working class, said Gramsci, "has, for reasons of submission and intellectual subordination, adopted a conception which is not its own but is borrowed from another group." In his book *History and Class Consciousness*, Hungarian Marxist Gregory Lukacs echoed, "in capitalism . . . economic factors are not concealed 'behind' consciousness but are present *in* consciousness itself (albeit unconsciously or repressed). . . . This leads to an antagonism between individual and class interests in the event of conflict . . . and also to the logical impossibility of discovering theoretical and practical solutions to the problems created by the capitalist system of production." Working-class consciousness would have to be raised.

The Frankfurt School, led by Marxists Max Horkheimer, Theodor Adorno, Herbert Marcuse, and Erich Fromm, imported this philosophy into the West wholesale. They also deepened the implications of the philosophy: If false consciousness could lead people to believe things they didn't actually believe, it could also cause people to define themselves in ways they didn't actually want to. False consciousness could corrupt one's whole self-definition. The only way to free oneself would be to break the shackles of the system entirely, thus unleashing a higher form of authenticity. For example, Fromm argued that the family provided an excellent example of the dangers of false consciousness eroding the *true* self. The family, says Fromm, "stamps its specific structure on the child." And that structure is dictated by capitalism.[5]

The concept of false consciousness has been adopted and utilized by every type of Scavenger.

For Looters, as we have seen, the capitalist system is to blame for people thinking individually.

For Lechers, the structures of family and church are to blame for the repressive inauthenticity by which most people lead their daily lives. Patriarchal systems have dictated how people think; as feminist Simone de Beauvoir writes in *The Second Sex*, women have become complicit in their own subjugation, thanks to the systems they accept almost naturally.[6]

The answer to this false consciousness, of course, is destruction of all institutions and norms, the sources of our repression. As Herbert Marcuse, an advocate of unreconstructed polymorphous perversity, argued, it was time for "the concept of a non-repressive civilization, based on a fundamentally different experience of being, a fundamentally different relation between man and nature, and fundamentally different existential relations."[7]

For Barbarians, it is the structures of the West that are to blame for a false consciousness among colonized peoples. Fanon, of course, was a Marxist, and argued that any domestic middle-class opposition to bloody revolution was a result of false consciousness; he also argued that colonialism had deracinated native peoples, and that only through bloody revolution could they remake themselves: "It has always happened in the struggle for freedom that such a people, formerly lost in an imaginary maze, a prey to unspeakable terrors yet happy to lose themselves in a dreamlike torment, such a people becomes unhinged, reorganizes itself, and in blood and tears gives birth to very real and immediate action."[8] Sartre argued that colonialism means that Europeans too are "estranged from ourselves."[9] Edward Said routinely wrote of alienation and problems of self-definition brought about by "Orientalism." The same is true for Coates, who lays all ideological problems at the feet of a powerful white supremacist structure.

Always and forever, for the Barbarians, individuals never have thoughts; their thoughts are merely the products of corrupt systems.

This is the highest form of the Great Conspiracy Theory possible.

You don't think what you think—you are merely a pawn.

You have been manipulated.

Which means that you must now see all your institutions wrecked, your civilization ground under bootheel, and your intellectual freedom restricted. Those who most passionately advocate against "false consciousness" invariably believe in compulsion of thought—in their own direction.

The Looters argue in favor of authoritarian control of thought in order to foreclose the possibility of reversion to the "capitalist mentality." This is why Soviet Russia ruthlessly quashed freedom of thought. As historian Robert Conquest writes regarding the Stalin era:

> To die, or lose your loved ones, is bad enough ... to be forced to denounce your father or husband, in the hope of saving the rest of the family, and, in general, to be compelled in public to express joy at the whole bloodbath, may be thought worse still. Truth almost perished. As the writer Isaac Babel remarked, "Today a man only talks freely to his wife—at night, with the blankets pulled over his head."[10]

George Orwell described the authoritarian rule of men's minds in *1984*, his terrifying allegory of tyrannical communism: "Asleep or awake, working or eating, indoors or out of doors, in the bath or in bed—no escape. Nothing was your own except the few cubic centimeters inside your skull."[11]

The Lechers are similarly uninterested in freedom of thought—they are interested in destroying the supposed systems of power so as to impose their own, which will supposedly "liberate" humanity from its chains. De Beauvoir, far from calling for the liberation of women's minds, called for a new system of power to be imposed from above in order to rewrite women's minds: "No woman should be authorized to stay at home to raise her children. Society should be totally different. Women should not have that choice, precisely because if there is such a choice, too many women will make that one. It is a way of forcing women in a certain direction."[12]

For Barbarians, freedom of thought is a tool to be utilized against the colonialist oppressors. None of the postcolonialists are in any way actively interested in freedom of thought in any of the "liberated" territories for which they so hotly advocate. Fanon never seemed to care whether freedom of thought would apply in a post-French Algeria; Said blamed the repressiveness of Arab tyrannies on the very presence of Israel in the Middle East and delusionally argued that a PLO-run state would be secular and democratic;[13] Coates has nothing to say about the tyranny and discrimination of Palestinian governance, but plenty to say about the only democratic state in the Middle East. The Barbarians have the unhappy habit of utilizing freedom of thought and openness to ideas in the West to argue for the overthrow of such freedoms everywhere else. And the academic Barbarians are more than happy to utilize their oppressor/oppressed matrix to bar those from academia who disagree—speech codes have long been a hallmark on college campuses, because to allow freedom of speech might threaten the ideological tyranny under which they operate.

RULE #2: THE PACK MUST DESTROY FREE MARKETS

If free minds cannot be trusted in a free system, the same holds true of free markets. This, of course, should not be a surprise: If free markets are all about innovation, and innovation is all about the wide distribution of knowledge—free minds—then of course free markets become the enemy of the Scavengers. As economist George Gilder correctly notes, "'The freer an economy is, the more this human diversity of knowledge will be manifested. By contrast, political power originates in top-down processes—governments, monopolies, regulators, and elite institutions—all attempting to quell human diversity and impose order. Thus power always seeks centralization."[14]

This next rule of the pack is simple: Free markets must be undermined.

For the pack, free markets act as an insult—a constant reminder that they are not Lions. As Eric Hoffer writes, "They want to eliminate free competition and the ruthless testing to which the individual is continually subjected in a free society."[15]

They must be undermined for two reasons, according to the Scavengers.

First, free markets must be undermined because they are *immoral*. Free markets are unjust, according to the Scavengers. They are unjust because success in a meritocracy is reliant on unearned qualities and capabilities. As a corollary to this argument, Scavengers further argue that free markets are unjust because, contrary to the logic of the Lions, hard work does not correlate with success.

Second, free markets are *degrading*, say the Scavengers. They reduce the eternal to the realm of the economic. "You're making everything about money!" they cry. In a better world, the Scavengers argue, the market wouldn't set the price of goods and services. Instead, the proper set of life values would dictate cost and availability.

Let's examine the cases, one by one.

The Moral Case Against Free Markets

According to the Scavengers, their own failure in the free market is not the result of any inherent lack of quality or effort. It is a result of the free market itself. Free markets, according to the Scavengers, are rigged—either in favor of those who have certain inborn qualities, or in favor of those who are born with certain advantages.

Now, it is certainly true that in any meritocracy, some will do better than others based on qualities for which they did not work. LeBron James did not work for his height or base athletic ability; I did not work for my inherent level of intelligence. Sure, both of us have worked to maximize those gifts. But we were not responsible for that with which we were born. Similarly, I did not work to be born into a solid two-parent family structure, with a loving mother and father. These imbalances are, of course, simple realities of life—but according to the Scavengers, they are a fatal flaw in the meritocracy.

Now, that isn't true. And anyone who has natural gifts would be a fool of the highest order to attribute those gifts to himself. At the same time, the imbalance of natural gifts is quite real. The same is true of the situations in which we are born—they are not of our own making, and they are inherently unequal. Must all such imbalances be corrected? If so, how? Opponents of free markets suggest that the quest for cosmic justice, in Sowell's felicitous phraseology, ought to be pursued through government coercion or reengineering—through force. Thus, per President Lyndon Baines Johnson in 1965:

> You do not take a person who, for years, has been hobbled by chains and liberate him, bring him up to the starting line of a race and then say, "you are free to compete with all the others,"

and still justly believe that you have been completely fair....
We seek not just legal equity but human ability, not just equality as a right and a theory but equality as a fact and equality as a result.[16]

Such a goal is utterly unachievable. In fact, coercive attempts to achieve "equality as a fact and equality as a result" have ended in immeasurable human suffering.

But do free markets have an answer for the inequalities among human beings?

As it turns out, they do.

Free markets correct for the imbalance of our natural gifts through the magic of *comparative advantage*. Trading the thing you are good at for the thing something else is good at is great for both sides; that's simply specialization. If you're good at making tennis balls and I'm good at making tennis rackets, it makes sense for us to trade. But comparative advantage makes a broader claim: that even if Party A is better at making tennis balls *and* rackets than Party B, it may make sense to specialize and then trade. That's because *time* matters. If Party A is more efficient at making balls than racquets, then an hour Party A spends making tennis balls is an hour not spent making rackets. This is called *opportunity cost*.

Think about your own life. You may be a smart person, perhaps a person capable of figuring out how to fix your toilet. But let's say you're a doctor, and you get paid $300 an hour to be a doctor. An hour you spend plumbing is an hour you're not doctoring. You're better off paying a plumber to spend two hours at $50 an hour to fix your toilet than spending one hour of your own time fixing your toilet.

This is why *trade* is an economic—and a moral—necessity. It is an economic necessity because you don't have unlimited time: If you couldn't trade based on comparative advantage, you'd be forced to do everything yourself. That would be quite expensive in terms of time; it would make your life materially worse. Today you can drop by a restaurant and buy a chicken-and-cheese sandwich with lettuce and tomatoes for $10, give or take. If you did it yourself from scratch—growing the wheat, slaughtering the chicken, making the cheese—as YouTuber Andy George has shown, it would take up to six months and $1,500.[17]

The exchange of goods, products, and services is, in fact, a form of innovation. No one invents anything on his own. The more networked humanity is, the faster innovation happens, and the faster it spreads. Comparative advantage means that the natural inequalities of mankind are actually *alleviated* by free markets—which is why everyone gets richer under capitalism, even if they do so at different rates. And it is why trade is a *moral* issue: If you prohibit people from freely controlling their labor and the products thereof, you damn them to a lifetime of unnecessary work.

The Spiritual Case Against Free Markets

Second, according to the Scavengers, free markets flatten the human soul.

As we've explored, free markets have inarguably bettered our world dramatically, increasing global prosperity and health exponentially everywhere they're tried.

So, how can the Scavengers argue against them?

They argue that markets aren't generating *true* value.

"A dive, a sunset, a joke: all can have an enormous amount of experiential value and no exchange value whatsoever," writes former Greek finance minister Yanis Varoufakis in *Talking to My Daughter About the Economy, Or, How Capitalism Works—and How It Fails*. "Anything without a price, anything that can't be sold, tends to be considered worthless, whereas anything with a price, it is thought, will be desirable." This, Varoufakis thinks, is one of the shortcomings of economics: It leaves out the human aspect of living. It reduces everything to a commodity. A more romantic view of life, taking into account the priceless nature of love and sunsets, might allow for a more just and rewarding distribution of resources.[18] This, in fact, is Marx's argument—he stated that without markets, which prize specialization, human beings would eventually be able to enjoy the fullest possible life:

> [I]n communist society, where nobody has one exclusive sphere of activity but each can become accomplished in any branch he wishes, society regulates the general production and thus makes it possible for me to do one thing today and another tomorrow, to hunt in the morning, fish in the afternoon, rear cattle in the evening, criticise after dinner, just as I have a mind, without ever becoming hunter, fisherman, herdsman or critic.[19]

Real value, in this viewpoint, is in the *experience of life*. And, they argue, no economic system that puts a price on such value can be truly effective. Teaching is more valuable than playing basketball; in fact, one could call education priceless. So why should we put a price on education? Our health is the most valuable thing we have. So we should we put a price on health care? Markets, even if they make things cheaper and better, also remove them of their deeper *meaning*. Better to declare priceless things a right and produce fewer of them than to declare them a commodity and produce more of them. We must protect our *true* values from the soulless nature of the pricing system.

This, of course, is a logical obfuscation. As Thomas Sowell points out, *all* values are noneconomic. Health care is priceless, and so is watching a sunset with your family. Economics and free markets aren't a way of determining the *absolute* value of any product, good, or service—such valuation isn't impossible. They are a way of weighing values *against each other*. There isn't enough health care, and there aren't enough sunsets with your family. Free markets create a mechanism for determining how to value one *against the other*.

Take, as the most obvious example, human life.

Now, in a cosmic sense, human life is priceless. But those who most frequently invoke the pricelessness of human life in order to undermine free markets certainly don't think human life is *literally* priceless. Lenin thought any economic system that put a price on life was somehow morally flawed—yet he called for mass murder in the name of his own system. More prosaically, human beings frequently undertake dangerous tasks in exchange for pay, or on behalf of an ideal. In fact, some of the greatest antagonists of the free market suggest that human life should be cut short on behalf of health care rationing by government. Princeton philosopher Peter Singer is admirably blunt: "The debate over health care reform in the United States should start from the premise that some form of health care rationing is both inescapable and desirable."[20]

When it comes to markets and morality, Sowell's explanation remains correct: "Market economies permit individuals to make decisions for themselves, based on their own moral values or other personal considerations—and at the same time the market forces them to pay the costs that their decisions create."[21] And Scavengers know this.

They know that life and sunsets aren't "priceless" in any real, practical sense. They simply argue against free markets because they don't like the prices attained *in the market*. In short, they would prefer to be in control of the distribution and production of everything. *Their values* should triumph, and theirs alone. If free markets take everyone's opinions into account, then free markets might act as a true measuring mechanism, determining who ought to make more or less, or what products ought to be more plentiful or scarce.

And *that* is precisely what the Scavengers cannot allow.

If free markets are a weighing machine, the Scavengers want to rig the scales.

The Scavengers' hatred of free markets forms its own Conspiracy Theory: that free markets are not in fact an evolutionary outgrowth of human nature over time, but an artificial creation by a self-protecting elite. This Conspiracy Theory is common to most of the Left and also part of the Right. Here, for the Left, is Bernie Sanders: "The goal of any democratic, moral, and rational system must be to create a society where people are healthy, happy, and able to live long and productive lives. . . . Our economic debates should not revolve around questions of resources. They should revolve around questions of intent, and will."[22] And here, for the Right, is Tucker Carlson: "Market capitalism is a tool, like a staple gun or a toaster. You'd have to be a fool to worship it. Our system was created by human beings for the benefit of human beings. We do not exist to serve markets. Just the opposite. Any economic system that weakens and destroys families is not worth having. A system like that is the enemy of a healthy society."[23]

Now, as we've explored, free markets aren't an arbitrary system consciously created "by human beings for the benefit of human beings" in the same way centralized economies are. Nobody sat down and constructed a "free market." Free markets are an evolutionary outgrowth of human autonomy and the private property that springs therefrom. You cannot reject free markets without rejecting their underpinnings: human creativity and innovation. No one is arguing that people ought to "worship" or "serve" markets, any more than people ought to worship or serve free speech—free speech is a system that simply recognizes human freedom, and large-scale attempts to interfere with that freedom end with disaster. Communities certainly can and should bar certain items from the marketplace itself—there are good cases that heroin and pornography ought to be illegal, for example. But markets aren't responsible for the prevalence of heroin and pornography any more than free speech is responsible for racial slurs.

Yet Sanders and Carlson seem to argue that economic debates aren't about efficient distribution of scarce resources, but about Deeper Moral Values™—again, suggesting that any outcome they do not like is the result of some purposeful plan designed to harm the people. With enough intent and enough will, free-market capitalism—the "enemy of a healthy society"—can be destroyed, and supplanted with something else. That something else has been, historically, central economic control. In the words of Benito Mussolini, "Man is man only by virtue of the spiritual process in which he contributes as a member of familial, social groups, the nation.... Fascism is therefore opposed to all individualistic abstractions based on eighteenth century materialism ... [and] does not believe in the possibility of 'happiness' on earth as conceived by the economic literature of the 18th century."[24]

It turns out that all too often, those who complain about the effects of free markets on the human soul are perfectly willing to use coercion to effectuate their own vision of the good—and to flatten millions of lives in the process.

RULE #3: THE PACK MUST DISINTEGRATE PUBLIC VIRTUE

Free minds and free markets, as we have discussed, must be supported by institutions that value and foster public virtue. Intermediate institutions such as families and churches provide the safety net for innovation and risk-taking; they provide the social fabric that binds us all together, and that unites us in our duties while maintaining our liberties. Our civilization is held up by those intermediate institutions.

It is no surprise, then, to find Scavengers seeking to disintegrate precisely those institutions. Churches and families must be destroyed. For where churches and families thrive in a free society, the West thrives; where churches and families decline, the West falls into decay.

For the Looters, public virtue acts as a palliative mechanism for capitalism—a balm that merely covers over the hideousness of free markets and thus must be abolished. As Sanders once told a charity ball in 1981, "I don't believe in charities." Sanders explained that the "fundamental concepts on which charities are based" were wrong, given that charity is rooted in private property. As he would later explain in his book *It's Okay to Be Angry About Capitalism*, "Real politics recognizes that the corporate elite are not nice guys, no matter how much they contribute to charity or how many awards they receive from universities and hospitals to which they have donated buildings. They are ruthless, and day after day they sacrifice human life and well-being in order to protect their privilege."[25]

Sanders is merely mirroring his Marxist forebears here. Marx and Engels were quite clear in their desire to wipe away every institution that could serve as a bulwark for private property—which is to say, virtually all intermediate institutions:

Law, morality, religion, are to [the proletariat] so many bourgeois prejudices, behind which lurk in ambush just as many bourgeois interests.... They have nothing of their own to secure and to fortify; their mission is to destroy all previous securities for, and insurances of, individual property.... The Communist revolution is the most radical rupture with traditional property relations; no wonder that its development involved the most radical rupture with traditional ideas.[26]

Unsurprisingly, the Soviet Union took this goal quite seriously.

From church to family, all intermediate institutions of society had to be destroyed. Lenin launched the so-called Godless Five-Year Plan, a campaign to destroy all vestiges of religion in Soviet society. Virtually all churches were shuttered. Stalin followed in Lenin's footsteps, proclaiming, "The Party cannot be neutral towards religion and does conduct anti-religious propaganda against all and every religious prejudice.... The Party cannot be neutral towards the bearers of religious prejudices, towards the reactionary clergy who poison the minds of the toiling masses. Have we suppressed the reactionary clergy? Yes, we have. The unfortunate thing is that it has not been completely liquidated."[27]

The traditional family met the same fate: All family was to be made secondary to the priorities of the state.

In 1932, the Soviet authorities began championing the myth of Pavlik Morozov, a thirteen-year-old boy so patriotic that he had denounced his own father to Soviet officials for corruption; his father was supposedly sentenced to ten years in a labor camp, and then subsequently death. After his father's execution, Pavlik's family supposedly decided to revenge themselves on him, and stabbed him to death. The

GPU—the predecessor of the KGB—then allegedly arrested the family members and executed *them*.

Pavlik was made a hero by the Soviets. Maxim Gorky, Soviet author and propagandist, wrote a piece printed across the Soviet Union championing him: "The struggle against small saboteurs—weeds and rodents—taught the children to counteract the large two-legged ones. Here it is appropriate to remember the feat of the Pioneer Pavel Morozov, a boy who understood that a man who is close to you by blood can easily be an enemy in spirit; for such a man we can have no mercy." He would later declare, "This little hero deserves a monument, and I am sure that a monument will be erected." He was made the subject of a film by famed director Sergei Eisenstein as well as a postage stamp. Never mind that the whole story was likely rooted in fiction.[28]

It should be treated as tautological that the Lechers must undermine public virtue. And they seek to do so in the most perverse of ways: by targeting children.

In July 2021, the San Francisco Gay Men's Chorus released a video on YouTube. The Chorus has a mission, according to its website: "We envision a world inspired and unified by the music we create.... We evolve society's views toward LGBTQ people through our commitment to excellence."[29] This commitment to excellence and evolution involves recruiting children to the cause, which is precisely what the SFGMC sang in their "Message from the Gay Community":

We're coming for them. We're coming for your children.
The gay agenda is coming home.[30]

This is called *liberation*, in the view of the Lechers.

The Lechers don't hide the ball in this regard. They believe with ardent fervor that they are doing a *favor* to children by exploding the roles, rules, and responsibilities designed to protect children historically. After all, the only way to create a society free of Western values is to indoctrinate young people before they can be shaped by intermediate institutions.

Take, for example, the shocking exponential multiplication of Drag Queen Story Hours and Family Friendly Drag Shows across the nation. Exposing children to cross-dressing men who twerk or gown-garbed dudes who read them books about gender fluidity—that's not just tolerant, it's now morally praiseworthy.

Why drag? Because drag is, by nature, violative. It is destructive: of gender, of tradition, of community. Violation is the essence of drag—which is precisely why drag used to be an edgy punch line. Violating norms in a society that respects norms is inherently funny. Bugs Bunny wore drag precisely because it was absurd, and transgressing social norms was worthy of laughter. Then drag queens became the face of social rebellion: They represented a challenge to the idea that men should not act like women, and vice versa.

As the Drag Queen Story Hour organization argues, such events are necessary in order to allow kids to "see people who defy rigid gender restrictions and imagine a world where everyone can be their authentic selves." This is the language of pure lechery: Your authentic self lies in your subjective sense of what you are—society must be reconstructed to cheer it. And, it goes without saying, if children are perceived as sexual beings, as many queer theorists argue, then that "authentic self" ought to be sexually informed and free too. Christopher Rufo correctly explains:

> After the norms of gender, sexuality, marriage, and family are called into question, the drag queen can begin replacing this system of values with "queer ways of knowing and being."[31]

Targeting children allows for the possibility of restructuring society. If institutions mold us—and if they have molded us in intolerant, bigoted ways—the only possibility of building a future free for transgressivism lies in conversion of the young, those who have not yet been touched by the impurity of tradition. This means first obliterating the intermediary institutions designed to protect children.

After all, the very concept of virtue is the enemy of the Lechers, who see those institutions as a threat to authenticity.

The mission to fight against traditional virtue begins with destroying the family; it extends to the church. As radical psychoanalyst Wilhelm Reich, a proponent of sexualizing children, wrote in 1945:

> The interlacing of the socio-economic structure with the sexual structure of society and the structural reproduction of society take place in the first four or five years and in the authoritarian family. The church only continues this function later. Thus, the authoritarian state gains an enormous interest in the authoritarian family. It becomes the factory in which the state's structure and ideology are moulded.[32]

If anything, the Lechers hate the family even more than the church. Feminist icon Betty Friedan famously characterized the role of the married American mother as "the comfortable concentration camp." Institutions like the family had turned women into "walking corpses."[33] No wonder feminist radical Shulamith Firestone called for the "tyranny of the biological family [to] be broken. And with it the psychology of power."[34]

As for the Barbarians, public virtue is merely a self-justifying Western pretense. There is no virtue in intermediate institutions—they merely maintain and strengthen the colonialist architecture. In particular, the Barbarian attacks the church rather than the family—families, of course, are common across culture, but the church is the core of the "colonial" ideology. Frantz Fanon calls Christianity "the implantation of foreign influences in the core of the colonized people.... The Church in the colonies is the white people's Church, the foreigner's Church. She does not call the native to God's ways but to the ways of the white man, of the master, of the oppressor. And as we know, in this matter many are called but few chosen."[35] Edward Said traces the evils of Orientalism back to its foundations: "the Church Council of Vienne in 1312."[36] In fact, says Said, the British used religion as a rationale for the usurpation of Muslim lands and authority.[37] Ta-Nehisi Coates, following the road paved by Marx, says that religion has been used by Americans to paper over America's racist history and present:

> You must resist the common urge toward the comforting narrative of divine law, toward fairy tales that imply some irrepressible justice.[38]

Of course, the result of all of this—the wiping out of intermediate institutions—is the predominance of the state. Intermediate institutions build the Pride; to tear down the Pride, the Pack must destroy those institutions. But anarchy is inherently unstable, unlivable. And so the state replaces those intermediate institutions with arbitrary power.

The Pack may call for anarchy when the Lions rule ... but the moment the Lions fall, the Scavengers centralize power in an arbitrary tyranny. The true alternative to intermediate institutions is not the Hobbesian state of nature, but the Leviathan. And in a world where the Leviathan is all, the only question is who will sit atop it, directing it against all enemies. Human beings are reduced to confusion and loneliness, made prey to an unending rootlessness that eventually voids itself in the comfort of the mob."[39]

RULE #4: THE PACK REJECTS EQUAL RIGHTS UNDER LAW

If the world is composed of systems of power, if failures are a result of those systems, and if those systems must be overthrown, then equal rights under law are not merely a sham—they *perpetuate the problem*. As Hayek correctly surmised, "To make people equal a goal of governmental policy would force government to treat people very unequally indeed."[40]

And indeed, this is what Scavengers insist must be done.

The Scavenger's logic is simple: for my friends, anything; for my enemies, the law.

The Scavengers argue that because the world is already rigged against some particular victim group, the only curative is unequal administration of justice—actual *injustice* in the name of a larger social end. After all, as LBJ's argument suggests, you can't line up everyone at the starting point in the race of life, set the rules—that everyone runs the same distance beginning at the same time—and then expect anything like a fair outcome. Some of the contestants will have been hampered by history, some by innate shortcomings; some will be victims of prior injustice, and some will be victims of the uneven distribution of resources natural to all social systems. Only a government of godlike powers can cure the injustices of life and guarantee cosmic justice. As LBJ explained in 1965: "The truth is, far from crushing the individual, government at its best liberates him from the enslaving forces of his environment."[41]

Not much has changed. The most recent defeated Democratic presidential candidate, Kamala Harris, stated while running for vice president in 2020, "There's a big difference between equality and equity. Equality suggests, 'Oh, everyone should get the same amount.' The problem with that, not everybody's starting out from the same place.... Equitable treatment means we all end up at the same place."[42]

Most blunt of all is Ibram X. Kendi, a racial Scavenger dedicated to the proposition that all of America's systems must be torn out at the root. Kendi argues that discrimination in the law is *mandatory* in order to establish true social justice: "The only remedy to racist discrimination is antiracist discrimination. The only remedy to past discrimination is present discrimination. The only remedy to present discrimination is future discrimination."[43]

For the Scavenger, unequal justice is *mandatory*, not optional.

By the logic of the Scavenger, guilt attaches to *persons*, not to acts.

If you oppose the Scavenger—if you uphold the system of Lions—you ought to be laid low.

No further information is necessary.

For Lenin, for example, the question wasn't due process of law, but coming up with a system that would penalize his enemies while sparing his friends. Senior Soviet leaders received dachas—small vacation homes in the country—with Lenin himself taking residence in a large dacha staffed with private cooks and servants;[44] enemies received a bullet to the back of the head. As he wrote in 1918, "the revolutionary dictatorship of the proletariat is ruled, conquered and maintained by the proletariat's violence against the bourgeoisie, unrestricted by any laws."[45] Soviet secret police leader Martin I. Latsis took Lenin's admonition quite literally, telling subordinates, "Do not seek in your accusations proof of whether the prisoner rebelled against the Soviets with guns or by word. First you must ask him to what class he belongs, what his social origin is.... These answers must determine the fate of the accused. That is the meaning of the Red Terror."[46]

Show trials and trumped-up evidence were the hallmarks of the Soviet system. Enemies of the regime—those who had "unfairly" benefited from the evil capitalist system, or who opposed the glorious rule of the Communist Party—were guilty by definition. Arbitrary arrest, detention, and execution were part and parcel of the true faith required by the quest for utopia.

True faith lay precisely in *rejecting* the rule of law.

Arthur Koestler describes the mindset in terrifying fashion in *Darkness at Noon*, his fictional take in 1940 on the trial and execution of an old Bolshevik condemned to death during Stalin's Great Purge. The main character, Nikolai Salmanovich Rubashov, is arrested by the secret police. He is accused of attempting to assassinate Stalin, a completely specious accusation. At first Rubashov fights the accusations during his interrogations. "I plead guilty to having rated the question of guilt and innocence higher than that of utility and harmfulness," he says. "Finally, I plead guilty to having placed the idea of man above the idea of mankind."

In the end, however, Rubashov must come to terms with the reality of his philosophy: If he protests his innocence, he sacrifices his entire ideology. He cannot hold to the importance of due process of law while simultaneously supporting Marxism. In this apotheosis, he finally recognizes that he must dismiss even his own innocence in favor of the cruel system to which he has devoted his life: "There is nothing for which one could die, if one died without having repented and unreconciled with the Party and the Movement. Therefore, on the threshold of my last hour, I bend my knees to the country, to the masses and to the whole people."[47]

This is the logic of the Looter. It is the logic of Bernie Sanders, who claims that "BILLIONAIRES SHOULD NOT EXIST."[48] It is the logic of the populist who claims that he ought to be able to redistribute earnings he has never created on behalf of certain segments of the population he happens to support—and who labels all those who oppose him "vicious" and "ruthless" and seeks rationale for their punishment.

The message of the Looter is the same as it has always been.

It is the message of Soviet secret police chief Lavrenty Beria: "Show me the man and I'll show you the crime."

For Looters, Lechers, and Barbarians, equal justice before law doesn't matter.

Not in the slightest.

Friends are privileged.

Enemies are guilty.

Thus the mechanisms of law enforcement have been turned against President Trump, who found himself on the wrong end of a wide variety of criminal cases and civil lawsuits—lawsuits often driven expressly by politics.[49] Thus the International Criminal Court has been hijacked by Barbarian activists: In 2024, the ICC issued a judgment against Israel's prime minister and defense minister for conducting a war against Hamas, accusing them of war crimes for waging a highly targeted antiterror campaign against an overtly genocidal enemy. Thus candidates for the Supreme Court like Brett Kavanaugh have been accused of heinous crimes without any supporting evidence, all in an attempt to prevent them from weighing in on contentious constitutional issues.

And thus criminals who meet particular intersectional standards are released onto the streets, to sin again. And thus massive riots are recast as "mostly peaceful" uprisings. And thus terrorist groups are portrayed as innocent victims. And thus equal justice before the law disappears—all in an attempt to overthrow meritocracy in favor of the arbitrary power games that characterize the way of the Scavenger.

The Nazis were sticklers for the rules.

From dress to language, they promulgated rules for every area of human life.

And they abided by the rules of the Scavenger with extraordinary alacrity and punctiliousness.

The Nazis cracked down on freedom of thought to the utmost extent. The Gestapo was every bit as vicious as the Soviet GPU or KGB; those who crossed the Nazi Party were deported or exterminated. Victor Klemperer, a Left-wing Jewish professor who somehow survived the Nazi regime while living in Dresden and kept a running diary, described the feeling:

> The never ending alarms, the never ending phrases, the never ending hanging out of flags, now in triumph, now in mourning—it all produces apathy. And everyone feels helpless, and everyone knows he is being lied to, and everyone is told what he has to believe.[50]

The Nazis, despite endless Marxist sermonizing to the contrary, similarly despised free markets. Hitler himself excoriated capitalism throughout his career. "Capitalism as a whole will now be destroyed," he shouted in 1922; "the whole people will now be free."[51] His viewpoint never changed; in 1941 he told the German people that the Nazis had defeated "capitalism and plutocracy."[52] Nazi Germany heavily regulated so-called private business, to the extent that businesspeople were essentially tools of the state. As German businessman Gunter Reimann wrote while laboring under Nazi rule, "You have no idea how far State control goes and how much power the Nazi representatives have over our work.... These Nazi radicals think of nothing except 'distributing the wealth.'"[53]

The Nazis, too, sought to override both church and family. Churches were made subject to the whims of the Nazi state; in 1935, for example, the Nazis arrested seven hundred pastors for reading protest statements from the pulpit.[54] As Hitler biographer Ian Kershaw writes:

> In early 1937, he was declaring that "Christianity was ripe for destruction" (Untergang), and that the Churches must yield to the "primacy of the state," railing against any compromise with "the most horrible institution imaginable."[55]

Hitler would spend most of his regime vacillating between a deep desire to crack down on churches and the reality that many Germans were religious Christians who objected to such heresies. While Hitler publicly embraced Christianity, according to historian Alan Bullock, "Once the war was over, he promised himself, he would root out and destroy the influence of the Christian Churches in Germany...."[56] Joseph Goebbels, Hitler's chief of propaganda, wrote in his diary in 1939, "The Führer is deeply religious, though completely anti-Christian. He views Christianity as a symptom of decay. Rightly so. It is a branch of the Jewish race. This can be seen in the similarity of their religious rites. Both (Judaism and Christianity) have no point of contact to the animal element, and thus, in the end they will be destroyed."[57]

For the Nazis, family structure also became secondary to the state. Forced sterilization and euthanasia in pursuit of racial purity was a hallmark of the regime. The *Lebensborn* program encouraged single Aryan women to be impregnated by Aryan men. Pregnant single women were taken to clinics, where they were indoctrinated in the ideology of the Fuhrer; the children produced to be raised by the state. Approximately 6,000 to 8,000 children were born to be raised by the Nazis under the program.[58] While the German government promoted a veneer of traditional family structure, the Nazis clearly oriented their policy toward a higher goal: the glorification of the state. If family structure came into conflict with the state, family would be ground beneath the heel. Heinrich Himmler explained, "Marriage in its existing form is the Catholic Church's satanic achievement; marriage laws are in themselves immoral.... with bigamy, each wife would act as a stimulus to the other so that both would try to be their husband's dream-woman."[59]

Most of all, the Nazi regime completely dismissed the notion of equality before the law. Membership in the Nazi Party carried with it privileges; placement in the Nazi hierarchy did the same. Status as a member of a despised class carried the penalty of death. As journalist William Shirer wrote, "The secret police announced that two men were shot for 'resisting arrest' yesterday.... Himmler now has power to shoot anyone he likes without trial."[60] As Shirer wrote in his seminal book *The Rise and Fall of the Third Reich*, "From the very first weeks of 1933, when the massive and arbitrary arrests, beatings and murders by those in power began, Germany under National Socialism ceased to be a society based on law. 'Hitler is the law!' the legal lights of Nazi Germany proudly proclaimed...."[61]

What justified all of these rules?

As always, the Great Conspiracy Theory, the same myth told over and over again since Cain and Able: the myth of the Haves and the Have-Nots, in which those who Have are the great oppressors of those who Have-Not. In 1942, Hitler spoke before the Reichstag, assuming new powers. He laid out his view of the civilizational conflict clearly and concisely:

> On one side we find the exponents of democracy, that is Jewish capitalism with all its deadweight of obsolete political theories and parliamentary corruption, its out-moded social order, the Jewish brain trust, the Jewish newspapers, stock exchanges and banks, a concern of mixed political and economic profiteers of the worst order, arm in arm with the Bolshevist state. Those powers of a perverted humanity are ruling, over them the Jew, who brandishes a bloody scourge in Soviet Russia. On the other side we find the nations who are fighting for their freedom and independence, who above all are fighting to assure the daily bread of their people. That is, the so-called Haves from the cellars of the Kremlin to the vaults of the banking houses in New York against the Have-Nots, that is those nations for whom a single bad harvest means privation and hunger....[62]

And all of this led, as both a by-product and end goal, to the worst targeted extermination of an ethnoreligious population group in all of human history.

After our visit to Auschwitz, I sit with Elon and we discuss the politics of the day before an audience of journalists. We have witnessed the site of the worst horrors humanity can unleash; that such horrors followed and relied upon a Scavenger ideology is no coincidence. I say to Elon that modern anti-Semitism is, at root, a conspiracy theory about power—it is an allegation that the losers in a meritocracy typically make regarding the winners. It is a claim that those who fail are somehow inherently victimized; that those who succeed are inherently oppressors.

And that perspective is both factually wrong and morally evil.

This should be fundamentally obvious.

It isn't.

But why isn't it? Why has the West become so vulnerable to the conspiracy theory of the Scavenger?

CHAPTER SEVEN

BLOODLUST AND BLOODGUILT

PHILADELPHIA

When Scavengers get their way, the result in the long run isn't merely chaos.

Chaos comes first.

Then there is one-party rule.

And finally, there is total enervation—a slide into stagnancy and decrepitude.

It is just a fourteen-minute drive from Independence Hall—where the American Founding Fathers pledged their lives, fortunes, and sacred honor in support of the Declaration of Independence, to the realization of a free and just America—to Hell.

Drive up the Interstate 95, exit at Westmoreland Street, then turn onto Kensington Avenue.

Kensington runs underneath the raised subway; every so often, the trains thunder and rattle overhead.

Nobody notices.

Nobody notices because Kensington Avenue is essentially a zombie apocalypse.

It is the worst thing I have ever seen in the United States.

We are here, in Kensington, to document the wages of the fentanyl crisis. It's a crisis that has killed hundreds of thousands of Americans. And we can see that crisis firsthand here, on the street.

Kensington Avenue runs for miles—and it's as busy as Forty-Second Street in New York. It isn't filled with tourists, though. People are shooting each other up with fentanyl, heroin, and tranq—a concoction of fentanyl laced with an animal tranquilizer called xylazine, designed to prolong the high of the fentanyl. Fentanyl is bad enough—a grain can kill you. The fentanyl crisis kills hundreds of thousands of Americans. Many of them die right here, on the streets of Philadelphia.

Tranq turns you into a living corpse.

We drive the streets, aghast at what we see. People, their legs or arms missing, feet without toes—all rotted away thanks to the tranq. People talking to themselves, babbling nonsensically as they scratch their festering bodies.

People bent at the waist, frozen, gazing into nothingness.

The pain that brought them to Kensington Avenue is no longer in their eyes.

Their eyes are just empty, almost lifeless.

We stop to speak with a local business owner. Her business can barely hold on: Rents in the area are so high that she lost her prior shop to a competitive bid—from a brothel, which did a cash business. The street is filled with prostitutes, trafficking their wares out in the open. Children walk to school past women selling their bodies.

We make a left onto a side street. Addicts hover over an open fire on the street. Up ahead, the road is blocked, flashing sirens warning us away. My security—all ex-police—tell me that the street has been blocked thanks to a homicide.

We make another left. Up ahead, the road is blocked . . . again. Another homicide, presumably.

As we drive past, the sounds of gunshots ring out.

This is what Hell looks like.

But amid all of this chaos, one particularly odd phenomenon pervades the place: silence. Societal breakdown is supposed to be loud, dangerous, shocking. But in Kensington, a wave of ennui has washed across the entire area.

No one cares.

People walk by the prone bodies of the infected or dying. Police officers wait on street corners near open solicitation for prostitution. Parents guide their children by homeless people shooting heroin into their feet—the veins in their arms and legs have already been too damaged for further use.

All of this was predictable.

Philosopher Soren Kierkegaard posited that *ressentiment* would level society—that the unique individual would be torn down to the ground in order to establish the superiority of the mass population. In passionate ages, he argued, new structures and ideas would be built, and the superior would be admired or at least grudgingly respected But in the stagnant society, the superior would be mocked and brought down to parity, and the result would be stagnation:

> The ressentiment which is establishing itself is the process of levelling, and while a passionate age storms ahead setting up new things and tearing down old, razing and demolishing as it goes, a reflective and passionless age does exactly the contrary:

it hinders and stifles all action; it levels.... At its maximum the leveling process is a deathly silence in which one can hear one's own heart beat, a silence which nothing can pierce, in which everything is engulfed, powerless to resist.[1]

But how do societies of Lions devolve so far?

How do the Scavengers—the inferiors of the Lions in their philosophy, their performance, and their systems—gain the upper hand?

THE GUILTY LION AND THE OPPORTUNISTIC SCAVENGER

The Scavenger is neither stronger nor wiser than the Lion.

The Scavenger has one tool, and one tool only: the decency of his enemy.

The Lion believes in sin—and those who believe in sin believe in guilt. Lions tend to believe, as Vasily Grossman writes in *Life and Fate*, that the difference between a good man and a bad man is that "a bad man will be proud all his life of one good deed—while an honest man is hardly aware of his good acts, but remembers a single sin for years on end."[2]

This rings true to those of us who believe in the notion of a God-ordered universe in which duties are owed to those around us—a universe of purpose. To Lions, guilt is a by-product of living in the world. In fact, feeling guilty is often a mark of virtue—the man who feels no guilt is widely (and correctly) perceived as either hubristic or amoral.

And it is *precisely* this guilt that Scavengers prey upon.

Guilt.

Bloodguilt.

In 1946, in the aftermath of World War II, anthropologist Ruth Benedict wrote a book titled *The Chrysanthemum and the Sword*. Benedict had a straightforward goal: to rip the lid off Japanese culture, to investigate "the most alien enemy the United States had ever fought in an all-out struggle." The Japanese, she noted, "are, to the highest degree, both aggressive and unaggressive, both militaristic and aesthetic, both insolent and polite, rigid and adaptable, submissive and resentful of being pushed around, loyal and treacherous, brave and timid, conservative and hospitable to new ways." What unifying feature could help define such a culture?

Benedict hit upon an idea to explain the contrast between Japanese culture and American culture. That idea was a distinction between what she termed cultures that "rely heavily on shame and those that rely heavily on guilt"—shame cultures versus guilt cultures.

Guilt cultures, Benedict argued, were most frequently present in societies that inculcated "absolute standards of morality" and relied on people "developing a conscience." Guilt is a private phenomenon: "In a nation where honor means living up to one's own picture of oneself, a man may suffer from guilt though no man knows of his misdeed and a man's feeling of guilt may actually be relieved by confessing his sin." America was an excellent example of a guilt culture.

Shame cultures, by contrast, are not interested in such internal questions. They are interested in how people are *perceived by others*. "True shame cultures," Benedict wrote, "rely on external sanctions for good behavior, not, as true guilt cultures do, on an internalized conviction of sin. Shame is a reaction to other people's criticism." Shame, in such cultures, "has the same place of authority ... that 'a clear conscience,' 'being right with God,' and the avoidance of sin have in Western ethics."[3] Japan, Benedict argued, was a prototypical shame culture.

In a conflict between shame cultures and guilt cultures, the most common pattern is misunderstanding: That which a member of a shame culture might find absolutely intolerable (losing face) may mean nothing to a member of a guilt culture, who might find the symbolism and show of shame cultures demeaning or foolish. Similarly, members of a shame culture may be bewildered by the ease with which members of guilt cultures dismiss shame—they might find such people rude and deem them ignorant.

Such misunderstanding can be bridged with time.

But there is another way in which such conflict can materialize: Shame cultures can read guilt cultures as inherently weak, and prey on them.

After all, one aspect of guilt culture, as we have explored, is the *necessity of guilt*. Guilt is unavoidable in a guilt culture. As Romans 3:23 posits, "all have sinned and fall short of the glory of God." In guilt cultures, confession of sin is seen as a mark of virtue—it is a recognition of our shortcomings, and a way of unburdening ourselves of our sins. In short, in guilt cultures, guilt is nothing to be ashamed of. In fact, it's often something to broadcast.

But in a shame culture, shame should be *avoided at all costs*. Shame can be avoided by secrecy; it can be avoided by submission to the group. Shame is not only unnecessary—it is a mark of inferiority.

This means that if members of a guilt culture admit their culpability—a mark of virtue and decency in a guilt culture—they will actually be *losing face and destroying their own credibility in a shame culture*.

This realization matters.

It matters an awful lot.

You may have recognized, by this point, that the way of the Lion is indeed a guilt culture. The Lion believes in absolute standards of morality. The Lion believes in the individual power to choose. The Lion believes in duty and sin and guilt—all of which apply, whether anyone else knows about them or not.

And you may have noticed that the way of the Scavenger is a shame culture.

The Scavenger does not believe in values—as we have explored, the Scavenger is willing to do anything to achieve power. The only standard is the arbitrary and moving standard of the Pack, enforced by power.

When Scavengers face down Lions, then, Scavengers have a weapon at their disposal: the virtue of the Lions. For if there is virtue, there is sin. Scavengers do not recognize the reality of sin—for Scavengers, sin does not exist as an independent concept in the world, but only as a useful way to mark transgression against the pack. Sin can be wielded as a weapon against Lions: Because Lions *do believe in sin*, Scavengers can accuse lions of sin, and Lions will *tend to believe them*—and to apologize, atone, and confess. Scavengers then use precisely that apology, atonement, and confession as the ammunition to destroy the Lions altogether. This is precisely why when Scavengers seek to destroy a Lion, they demand an apology—and why the worst thing a Lion can do is apologize to a Scavenger. What follows such an apology isn't forgiveness, but destruction.

Because the Lion abides by a Higher Law, the Scavenger uses the Higher Law against him: The Scavenger violates the Higher Law, tramples on it, spits on it, but demands that the Lion continue to uphold it. Because the Higher Law is a boundary on the power of the Lion—because the Lion feels guilty if he fails to uphold the Higher Law—the Lion is vulnerable to its invocation; the Scavenger, shameless and brutal, never is.

The Scavenger points to the Higher Law and says, "Look, you have violated this law. You ought to feel guilt."

The Lion listens. And the Lion submits.

The Lion submits because the West has become, in narcissistic and navel-gazing fashion, *obsessed* with its own guilt. Failing to recognize that sin is universal but that good is exceptional, the West has instead fallen for the trap of linking its own unique good with unique sin: If the West is more powerful and prosperous than its enemies, that must be because its sins are unique. This is precisely the case the Scavengers make. In the words of deconstructionist Jacques Derrida, "[I]t must be cried out, at a time when some have the audacity to neo-evangelize in the name of the ideal of a liberal democracy that has finally realized itself as the ideal of human history: never have violence, inequality, exclusion, famine, and thus economic oppression affected as many human beings in the history of the earth and of humanity."[4]

Because the Lions are successful, the Scavengers argue, they bear unique bloodguilt.

And because the lions bear unique bloodguilt, their repentance must be unique, as well: They must surrender. As French philosopher Pascal Bruckner writes:

> [T]he duty to repent forbids the Western bloc, which is eternally guilt, to judge or combat other systems, other states, other religions. Our past crimes command us to keep our mouths closed. Our only right is to remain silent.... Reserve and neutrality will redeem us. No longer participating, no longer getting involved in the affairs of our time, except perhaps by approving of those whom we formerly oppressed.[5]

Shelby Steele, a black radical who would later become politically conservative, recalls just this attitude from the aging Lions of the universities. In the 1960s, Steele relates, he led black students into the office of the university president to make a series of absurd demands. "[W]ith all the militant authority I could muster," Steele writes, "I allowed the ashes from my lit cigarette to fall in little grey cylinders onto the president's plush carpet. This was the effrontery, the insolence, that was expected in our new commitment to militancy." Steele fully expected the college president to rise to the challenge. But instead, the Lion bowed before the Scavenger: "I saw something like real anger come over his face, and he grabbed the arms of his chair as if to spring himself up.... But his arms never delivered him from his seat." The university president's own "vacuum of moral authority"—at least his perception of guilt—prevented him from standing up for his institution, for his civilization.[6]

This is how the civilization of Lions falls.

THE END OF WESTERN INNOVATION

In the free market, the meritorious win; the Lions prosper.

The Scavengers lose.

They lose ... unless they can convince the Lions that their very success, their very prosperity, is a mark of sin.

Indeed, this is precisely the goal of the Scavenger.

In order to achieve this, the Scavenger could convince the Lion that he has *deprived* others of the opportunity to prosper—that the economy is a zero-sum game in which all wealth is achieved through exploitation. This, indeed, is a common tactic used by demagogic politicians. The inveterately imbecilic Representative Alexandria Ocasio-Cortez (D-NY) uses such tactics routinely; she told Ta-Nehisi Coates in 2019, "I do think a system that allows billionaires to exist when there are parts of Alabama where people are still getting ringworm because they don't have access to public health is wrong."[7] Here she lays out the idiot's case that prosperity is in and of itself sinful: the implication that billionaires somehow get rich by impoverishing poor ringworm victims in Alabama.

The problem with this argument is that it is obviously untrue.

In fact, few Scavengers make the zero-sum argument openly these days.

Instead, today's Scavengers have an alternative tactic: They accuse the lion of *selfishness* and *arrogance*.

The Lions, they say, are selfish for not giving *more*.

And the Lions, they say, are arrogant for believing that they deserve what they have earned.

"Sure," says the Scavenger, "you didn't steal your money. But you *are* cruel, arrogant, ungenerous . . . unless you turn over your wealth to us. *We* allow you to succeed. And *we* are the many. How much wealth do you *need*? Why don't you just pay your *fair share*?"

Everyone could always give more to charity, work more hours, donate more time, pay more taxes. While capitalism isn't a zero-sum game, charity *is*: If I'm not giving charity, the potential charity recipient isn't receiving it. So long as charity is seen as good (which it is), it isn't difficult for Scavengers to turn the charitable impulse—and failure to satisfy it—against the Lion.

This is particularly true when combined with the argument, made by Scavengers, that wealth isn't a result of innovation or hard work, but a sort of lucky strike made by a fortunate few, who have benefited from the unrewarded labor of others. "There are a lot of wealthy, successful Americans who agree with me—because they want to give something back. They know they didn't—look, if you've been successful, you didn't get there on your own.... If you've got a business, you didn't build that," said Barack Obama.

"I'm a capitalist. But just pay your fair share," said Joe Biden.

These are appeals directed to the virtues of the Lion.

To their purported sin and guilt.

It is this guilt upon which the Scavengers rely.

And it works. As Thomas Sowell writes, "Worst of all, guilt has so furtively stolen into many hearts and minds that people feel apologetic about being civilized, educated and productive when others are barbaric, uneducated and parasitic. When civilization apologizes to barbarism, something has gone very wrong at a very fundamental level."[8]

There is a group chat to which I am a party, populated largely by some of the wealthiest and most successful company founders in America. During the last election cycle, a conversation began between these billionaires about Kamala Harris's proposed wealth tax. The conversation quickly turned into a competitive virtue-signaling session, with various billionaires trying to explain just why they could convince Harris and her allies that if they pledged to pay a certain percentage, the Scavengers would *understand* that they weren't greedy and selfish and arrogant.

To which I responded, "Good luck."

The Scavenger's promise of absolution is, of course, a lie.

Scavengers embrace the uncompromising religion of envy, which offers no absolution.

But Lions may pursue the illusion anyway. In the words of Helmut Schoeck, author of *Envy: A Theory of Social Behavior*: "In the twentieth century, too, for the first time, certain societies have grown rich enough to nourish the illusion that they can afford the luxury of buying the good will of the envious at ever steeper prices."[9]

But it won't work.

If these Lions lie down before the Scavengers, the Scavengers do not forgive and forget. They instead demand more from them—and any denial of such demands would draw even sharper attack. The best a tamed Lion can hope for is to be used as a counterexample to the other Lions—the "good" billionaire, who makes the right noises, may be allowed a temporary respite from the razor teeth and claws.

A *temporary* respite. Because sooner or later, even the "good" Lion will be ravaged by the Scavenger when he is no longer useful.

This is true for all those who make provision for the Scavenger, hoping for mercy.

The Scavenger *always* meets weakness with murderous action ... eventually.

Franz von Papen was a German diplomat and battalion commander of supposedly unimpeachable character and moderate conservative credentials. As the leader of the so-called Center Party in Germany, he represented a shrinking party—but one with its hand on the tiller of state. As Hitler's Nazi Party rose, Papen was asked by President Paul von Hindenburg, the most beloved military leader of his era, to become chancellor. His chancellorship was marked by increasing centralization of power, but shrinking popularity; in 1932 he was replaced by the man who had helped make him chancellor, Kurt von Schleicher.

Papen, who believed himself superior to Schleicher, made a last-ditch gambit for power. He went to Hindenburg and asked Hindenburg to make Hitler chancellor of Germany, with himself as vice chancellor. Supposedly the new Hitler cabinet would moderate the Nazi leader.

That is not what happened.

As Hitler consolidated power in his cabinet, marginalizing all of Papen's allies, Papen began to chafe. In June 1934, he delivered a speech at the University of Marburg, where he criticized Hitler's excesses and called for a restoration of historic German freedoms. In particular, Papen tore into the SA—the *Sturmabteilung*, the paramilitary wing of the Nazi Party, run by the vicious Ernst Rohm—and said that their "second revolution" was characterized by "selfishness, lack of character, insincerity, lack of chivalry, and arrogance." The so-called Marburg speech enraged Hitler; it became shockingly popular, and began to sow seeds of discontent with Hindenburg.

And so Hitler acted.

On June 30, 1934, Hitler initiated the so-called Night of the Long Knives. The SS and Gestapo, at Hitler's behest, proceeded to murder all of Hitler's closest competitors and enemies, including Rohm, Nazi rival George Strasser, Schleicher, and all of Papen's top aides, including Edgar Jung, who had authored the Marburg speech.[10]

Papen himself was kept under house arrest; he thought that he himself might be killed.

He was not. Instead, he resigned from the government.

But within a month, he accepted a post from Hitler as German ambassador to Austria, where he would help usher in the German annexation of the country, the Anschluss.

After the war, Papen would end up tried at Nuremberg and acquitted of charges, but then condemned to an eight-year sentence by a German denazification court.

The tamed Lion may be eaten last, but he will undoubtedly be eaten.

THE END OF WESTERN VICTORY

In direct and open wars between Lions and Scavengers, Lions almost always win.

That is because Lions are warriors, while Scavengers are cowards.

Yet Scavengers *can* win, and increasingly *do* win. All they have to do is convince the Lions *not to win*.

And indeed, this is precisely what the Scavengers have done: They have used the laws of war against those who wrote them.

Such restrictions on the ways of war have developed over centuries in order to restrict the power of the Lion, to keep the Lion from destroying all around him in pursuit of victory. The Geneva Conventions, for example, were established originally in 1864 by twelve European states; the goal was for member parties to treat wounded and captured soldiers humanely, and to allow third-party humanitarian groups and civilian groups to aid the wounded. The Conventions were expanded in 1906, and then again in 1949, after the horrors of World War II. The Conventions of 1949 were expanded in order to protect civilians in war zones. One of the obvious goals of the Conventions was to grant protection to soldiers in uniform, and to civilians out of uniform.

All of which is praiseworthy, of course.

But such restrictions can also be used by Scavengers in order to destroy the Lion.

In fact, it is precisely this tactic that has been perfected over the course of decades by Scavengers everywhere. Relying on the Lions to abide by a more humane war code, the Scavengers exploit that same code: If the Lion worries about killing too many civilians, the Scavenger cloaks himself as a civilian while engaging in military activity; if the Lion is concerned about collateral damage, the Scavenger seeks to maximize civilian casualties so as to magnify that concern; if the Lion seeks to pacify the local population via positive incentives, the Scavenger seeks to maximize the suffering of that local population to magnify threat. The Lion is forced to play defense rather than to attack, bound by his adherence to a code the Scavenger denies but insists that the Lion apply, no matter the circumstances.

This spells defeat, for half measures cannot be pursued in war. War is hell, and it is meant to be. Only when the losing side discovers just how hellish war is does it surrender. Machiavelli explains in *The Discourses* that the Romans "avoided always the mid-way" in effectuating judgment on the conquered: Those whom they pardoned, they loaded with benefits; those who chose not to join then were punished with severity. To do otherwise, Machiavelli says, is to hand victory to the enemy, who feels no obligation to any Higher Law: "it is more honorable for a Prince to extirpate them quite at once, than to endeavour to preserve them with a thousand difficulties and dangers."[11]

If abiding by the Higher Law means defeat, the Higher Law becomes irrelevant—for if the Lion falls, so too does that Higher Law. It does the Higher Law no service for the Scavenger to rule. As Thomas Jefferson put it, "A strict observance of the written law is doubtless one of the high duties of a good citizen, but it is not the highest. The laws of necessity, of self-preservation, of saving our country when in danger, are of higher obligation. To lose our country by a scrupulous adherence to the written law, would be to lose the law itself, with life, liberty, property and all those who are enjoying them with us; thus absurdly sacrificing the ends to the means."[12] When Abraham Lincoln suspended the writ of habeas corpus during the Civil War in order to allow for the arrest without due process of insurrectionists, he explained, "Are all the laws, but one, to go unexecuted, and the government itself go to pieces, lest that one be violated?"[13]

This is the Lion at war.

But the Lion, fearing his own dominance, opens himself up to precisely the guilt the Scavenger seeks from him. The Lion, too successful against the Scavenger, begins to wonder at his own brutality, at the darkness he must unleash in order to secure victory. If the Lion falls prey to the lies of the Scavenger, the Lion then makes a crucial civilization error: He begins to believe that war need not be cruel or brutal at all, and that only an antiseptic war that prevents literally all harm to civilians can be fought. If the Lion falls short of perfection, he deems himself guilty. And the Scavenger, recognizing this mistake, fights the dirtiest war imaginable, hiding behind civilians, blaming the Lion when civilians are killed—and maximizing the Lion's guilt.

This guilt is helped along by the Barbarian mythmaking of the Scavenger, who suggests that he has no independent motivation of his own—that his own violence, cruelty, and evil are simply a result of the overwhelming power of the Lion. The Scavenger pretends that he is a victim, as always, and that his own brutality and barbarity are a response to the Lion; if only the Lion would stop defending himself and his pride, all war would cease. This is the argument made by Noam Chomsky, who rarely met a dictator he would not defend. Chomsky has spent decades savaging America while suggesting that her enemies were justified by America's vile actions abroad. Comparing American pretensions to those of the Nazis and Japanese fascists, Chomsky writes:

> [The American foreign policy record] would get any other country labeled a terrorist state.... When populations around the world are surveyed, they have ranked the United States as a greater threat to world peace and democracy than Russia or China. Much that is documented here has long been obvious to the victims of American aggression. They can only laugh when they hear US presidents speak of the country's commitment to humane values.[14]

He goes on to say that, as it turns out, virtually every evil in every conflict, ranging from Vietnam to 9/11, from Chinese aggression to Palestinian terrorism to Russian expansionism, is a "predictable consequences of our actions."[15]

If you believe the Scavengers, the only corrective is surrender or suicide. Chomsky proposes a vision of "no military alliances, no victors and defeated, common efforts to create a kind of social democratic future."[16]

This may be catnip for the naïve—or for the attendees of my group chat. It is suicidal in practice.

The only way for the Lion to defeat the Scavenger is to ignore his lies: to understand that the Scavenger is indeed barbaric, dishonest, and cruel—and to recognize that victory requires the Lion to do the dark things in the night he would never contemplate in any other circumstances.

The Lion must fight, or else the Lion effectively commits suicide.

And the Scavengers are happy to assist in the Lions' euthanasia.

THE END OF WESTERN VALUES

Lions have one strength, above all: the strength of their values, and the social fabric built therefrom. Scavengers cannot defeat the pride; they must instead find a way to separate the Lions from one another, making them vulnerable.

To do that, the Scavengers prey on yet another virtue of the Lion: mercy.

Social cohesion relies on the balance between prudence and mercy, as we have discussed. Prudence suggests the dangers of radical change, and requires that everyone play by the rules; it is innately bound up with justice. Mercy allows those who have sinned to rectify their sin, to remain part of the community so long as they do not threaten the fabric of the community.

The Scavenger, however, says that the Lion is insufficiently merciful.

Unkind.

Intolerant.

The Scavenger insists that the Lion provide mercy under all circumstances, even when totally undeserved. The Scavenger insists that no matter his own evil decisions, any lack of success deserves mercy; that mercy is a quality to be lauded even when misdirected. In fact, the Scavenger goes further: The Scavenger lies, and argues that his own failures are the fault of the Lion, so that the Lion isn't even providing mercy, but reparation.

The Lion knows the falsity of this view. To incentivize the Scavenger in his evil is to strengthen that evil. Mercy to the exploitative is cruelty to the decent. "Mercy on sinners," says Maimonides, "is cruelty to all creatures."

But the Lion forgets. The very quality that leads Lions to be Lions—a self-critical perspective that allows the Lion to grow from his mistakes—is susceptible of perversion: deconstructing oneself in pursuit of a ritualistic self-glorification. As Bruckner correctly notes, "Self-denigration is all too clearly a form of indirect self-glorification. Evil can come only from us; other people are motivated by sympathy, good will, candor. This is the paternalism of the guilty conscience: seeing ourselves as the kings of infamy is still a way of staying on the crest of history."[17]

This means that if you wish to defeat the Lion, the best way to do so is to play victim.

And this is precisely what the Scavenger does.

The Scavenger declares that his own vices must be either ignored or celebrated. Failure to do so means that the Lion is cruel and nasty. Only one small trick is required in order to transmute sin into virtue: membership in a victim group. Now, typically, membership in a victim group requires that you be targeted for *no good reason*; usually this means that you are being targeted because of an immutable characteristic. Racism, for example, is wrong because it is discrimination based on something you cannot change and that is irrelevant to behavior. Not all discrimination is wrong—this is why we use the term *discriminating* to describe good taste. Only *baseless discrimination* is wrong: discrimination against someone based on group membership despite evidence that such membership has no bearing on relevant behavior.

But the Scavenger goes further. The Scavenger makes the argument that *any discrimination is wrong*. Discrimination is de facto evidence of evil. If you discriminate against *behavior*, that too is now considered the worst sort of discrimination. If you oppose devotees of an ideology that mandates pagan child sacrifice, for example, this is now considered *divisive intolerance*.

Take, for example, the grooming-gangs scandal in England.

Over a period of decades, Muslim immigrants to multiple cities throughout the United Kingdom formed rape groups: groups of men who would groom young white girls by offering them alcohol and food, seduce the underage girls into sex, and then pass them around these groups to be raped. The crime was not rare; it spanned the country, from Rochdale to Rotherham, from Oldham to Oxford. Thousands upon thousands of young girls were treated as chattel, in the most vicious possible way.

And the police and the politicians and the press did nothing.

How did this happen?

It happened because elites in the West were invested in a narrative of moral equivalence—that all cultures were equal, and that to stand up for the proposition that some cultures are superior to others would be to engage in the sin of racism and Islamophobia. The alternative—a brutal rejection of multiculturalism and an assessment that some cultures are, in fact, superior to others—became unthinkable. Journalist Andrew Norfolk, who broke the scandal in *The Telegraph*, acknowledges clearly that he knew about the situation years earlier, but refused to report on it for precisely such reasons: "I remember so clearly the feeling of how on earth do you report a story that is a fantasy for the far right? It's everything you could wish for if you were pushing a particular agenda. It's innocent white girls and it's evil dark-skinned men.... To my shame, I allowed my liberal fear about giving succor and credence to the British National Party to act as a brake on actually doing my job."[18]

The grooming-gangs scandal in England was a perfect materialization of Frantz Fanon's threats of rape against colonizers, combined with Jean-Paul Sartre's prophecy of colonial peoples imported into the heart of the West.

And the West performed its part to a T.

The West's enemies know all of this.

They use it.

This is why Shabir Ahmed, one of the men tried and found guilty of child rape, appealed his sentence to the European Court of Human Rights in 2016 by claiming that he was a victim of racism in violation of human rights law.

He explained, "It's become fashionable to blame everything on Muslims these days."[19]

Islamophobia has become a shield for the worst behavior on the planet. It is a call for mercy from those who have none for others. As Salman Rushdie, victim of an Islamic fatwa that resulted in his near murder, wrote:

> A new word had been created to help the blind remain blind: Islamophobia. To criticize the militant stridency of this religion in its contemporary incarnation was to be a bigot. A phobic person was extreme and irrational in his views, and so the fault lay with such persons and not with the belief system that boasted over one billion followers worldwide.[20]

The claim of Islamophobia is merely one of the calls for mercy made by Scavengers. Those who maintain that boys and girls cannot transmute into one another are termed *transphobes*, deemed cruel and intolerant. Those who oppose drag queens reading stories about lesbian marriage to children are deemed *homophobes*. This game has become de rigueur for Scavengers—after Iran spent decades spreading terrorism and violence throughout the Middle East and beyond, its new president claimed that reports of its evil were mere "propaganda" and a reflection of "Iranophobia."[21]

The Lion only falls for this game because he does not have the strength of his convictions—the willingness to drop the niceties and declare some behaviors, cultures, and ideas *worse*. Quite often, the Lion avoids just that argument out of fear of hypocrisy—fear that the Scavenger will call out his own sins. This was the argument of Ahmed, who shouted in court that his grooming group should not be blamed because British society had left white girls vulnerable. He screamed:

> We are the supreme race, not these white bastards.... You destroyed my community and our children. None of us did that. White people trained those girls to be so much advanced in sex.[22]

The Lion must defend his own values. And that requires declaring—correctly—the values and behavior of the Scavenger *inferior*.

HOW SCAVENGERS CONSOLIDATE CONTROL

It does not require a majority of a population of Scavengers for the Scavengers to take control. It requires only a dedicated core group and a large majority of vacillating Lions unwilling to stand up and roar.

All too often, the conditions for such coups are ripe. It does not take much hectoring for many Lions to go silent in the face of the Scavengers. It does not require much of a push for many Lions to engage in a masochistic self-reflection that offers the promise but not the reality of absolution.

Then the Scavengers can *truly* take control.

If the root argument of the Scavenger is that they are victimized by a Great Conspiracy Theory, the failures of the Scavenger in governing a society actually *help the Scavenger*. Scavengers gain power by claiming that society has been controlled by a caste of vicious men seeking to keep them down. Once they gain power, Scavengers consolidate power in order to "destroy" those men. In the process, they maximize their own discretionary and arbitrary power. As Karl Popper explains, this leads to a self-reinforcing cycle of ever-greater control and ever-greater failure:

> The use of discretionary powers is liable to grow quickly, once it has become an accepted method, since adjustments to discretionary short-term decisions can hardly be carried out by institutional means. This tendency must greatly increase the irrationality of the system, creating in many the impression that there are hidden powers behind the scenes, and making them susceptible to the conspiracy theory of society with all its consequences—heresy hunts, national, social, and class hostility.[23]

Thus, a vicious loop is created.

Step 1: The Scavenger claims victimhood at the hands of the Great Conspiracy Theory.

Step 2: The Scavenger gains control by sidelining the Lions.

Step 3: The Scavenger declares that the only way to end the Great Conspiracy Theory is to use arbitrary power to root out the demonic caste in charge, and centralizes even more control.

Step 4: When the Scavenger fails to heal social ills, revert to Step 3.

The Kensington neighborhood of Philadelphia has been Democrat-governed for decades. At no point have its leaders acknowledged their failures. Instead they blame the "system" and demand more power in order to fix a problem they only intensify. The same is true in Los Angeles, Chicago, Detroit, and other failing American cities.

This vicious loop can only be broken by the strength of the Lion.

That is why it is a top priority for Scavengers to break any and all remaining Lions using the power they have aggregated. If ever Lions rise—if ever they demonstrate that success is not barred by the Great Conspiracy Theory, that success and failure are largely in the hands of the individual in a free society—the entire system comes undone.

The Scavengers *must defend the failing system.*

They *must exacerbate it.*

And they must destroy anyone who gets in their way.

Kensington is a failure because of the vicious loop.

It was a normal working-class community as late as the 1950s, with large industries ranging from textiles to shipbuilding and fishing. Over the course of the 1930s, the FDR administration's attempts to spread unionization bore extraordinary fruit in Philadelphia; some four in ten Philadelphians worked manufacturing jobs by the 1950s, and three-quarters were union members.[24] Large-scale unionization efforts were driven by a Great Conspiracy Theory—that employers were depriving workers of their hard-earned wages through collusive efforts, and that government-sponsored unionization would pry more money out of those employers.

That Conspiracy Theory collapsed in the 1960s, when the bloated price of labor in manufacturing areas of Philadelphia turned industrial areas into ghost towns. Major firms left the area entirely, or went out of business thanks to external competition. During the period from 1970 to 2000, Philadelphia shed full-time jobs to the tune of 23 percent. As businesses fled, the Scavengers in government promised more social services, paid through more taxes. The city of Philadelphia raised its "temporary" 1.5 percent wage tax, instituted in 1939, to nearly 5 percent by the mid-1990s. As the Center City District & Central Philadelphia Development Corporation reports, "[L]ocal tax policy exacerbated the push to the suburbs since business and residents with choice could easily avoid these taxes by moving out of the city. From 1970 to 2014, the city's regional employment share fell from 45% to 24%." Employment dropped. School funding dropped.

The city emptied out.

And the streets became a wasteland.

As of 2017, Philadelphia had the worst adult and child poverty rates and lowest median income of the 25 most populous counties in the United States. In Kensington, the poverty rate stood at above 40 percent.[25] Population in Philadelphia overall dropped from 2 million in 1950 to approximately 1.5 million in 2019.

Philadelphia has not had a Republican mayor since 1952.

And Kensington is a hellhole.

There is only one way for Kensington to heal: restoration of all the things that the Scavengers reject. Kensington must again embrace free markets, public virtue, rule of law. No substitute will do; mercy for the

Scavengers who currently plague Kensington, from the drug pushers and pimps to the politicians who defend them, will end with more suffering.

The Lion must renounce his supposed guilt.

The Lion must roar.

CHAPTER EIGHT

THE LION ROARS

The Scavengers crowd around the battered Lion.

Our institutions lie in ruins; our borders in tatters; our communities in knots.

The Lion, weary from the exertions of the centuries, bleeds.

The Scavengers snarl and circle him.

The dream of the Scavenger, it seems, will finally come true.

The Lion, it seems, will finally die.

And then it emerges.

It emerges from the belly of the Lion: a low grumbling at first.

It resonates in the Lion's throat, growing louder with each passing millisecond.

And then, at last, the Lion opens his massive jaws.

He struggles to his feet.

And he roars.

His strength, dormant for so long, still rests coiled in his limbs.

His courage still beats in his chest.
The Lion's honor is not dead after all.

BUENOS AIRES, ARGENTINA

Argentina is a gorgeous country.

Stretching from the tropics down to the sub-Antarctic, Argentina contains some of the world's greatest natural beauty, from the Andes Mountains to the Perito Moreno Glacier of Argentina.

It is also one of the world's greatest stagnation stories.

I am in Buenos Aires to speak to one of the first large conventions of conservatives in the country's modern history, and to meet with the new president of the country, Javier Milei. Once upon a time, Argentina was one of the richest countries in the Western Hemisphere. In the early twentieth century, Argentina was one of the ten richest countries on the planet on a per capita basis; in 1913 it was wealthier by that metric than France or Germany.[1] Blessed with abundant natural resources, Argentina's economy exploded thanks to the imposition of Western-style governmental institutions: From 1870 to the turn of the century, Argentina grew at one of the world's fastest clips.

And then it all went wrong.

In 1916, Argentina elected a radical Leftist government.

In 1930, the government was overthrown by a military coup, with the new regime modeling itself on Mussolini.

In 1946, after a countercoup, General Juan Peron took power.

The earlier coup and countercoup, combined with the effects of the Great Depression, led Argentina down a path toward economic chaos. Peronism, however, crippled the Argentine economy beyond all recognition.

Now, as we drive through Buenos Aires, the poverty is evident to the naked eye. Huge slums now pockmark the city, known as *la miseria*: enormous shantytowns made of rudimentary materials, connected illegally to power sources via extension cords, without running water or sewage systems. Drug gangs have historically controlled many of these neighborhoods, leaving chaos and violence in their wake.[2]

Argentina's history of instability has wreaked havoc on the country's finances: Inflation averaged nearly 200 percent annually from 1944 to 2024.[3] The consequences have been disastrous: The country has defaulted on its debt nine times.

And that means suffering.

This is what happens when the Pack takes over.

In 1960, Argentine poet and author Jorge Luis Borges penned a short story titled "The Mountebank." In it, he describes the arrival of a mysterious stranger in a small village on the Chaco River. The man proceeds to set up a fake coffin, complete with a mannequin inside. The villagers, believing the man to be important, file by and offer him condolences. Borges writes, invoking the hideous populism of Juan and Eva Peron:

> Perón was not Perón, either, nor was Eva, Eva—they were unknown or anonymous persons (whose secret name and true face we shall never know) who acted out, for the credulous love of the working class, a crass and ignoble mythology.[4]

The Scavengers have ruled Argentina for decades.

But something has changed in Argentina.

The Lion is roaring again.

Javier Milei is a unique politician. He didn't start off in politics; he started off in economics, after an itinerant career as a rock musician and soccer goalie. In 2020 he formally ran for office, running on the slogan, "I didn't come here to lead sheep, but to awaken lions." In 2023 he ran for president of Argentina, carrying a chain saw to signify the cuts to government he would pursue, shouting "¡Viva la libertad, carajo!"

And he won.

Standing before the Casa Rosada in December 2023, he said:

For more than one hundred years, politicians have insisted on defending a model that only produces poverty, stagnation, and misery. A model that assumes that citizens exist to serve politics, not that politics exists to serve citizens. A model that considers the task of a politician to be to direct the lives of individuals in all possible spheres and areas. A model that considers the state as a spoil of war to be shared among friends. Ladies and gentlemen, this model has failed.

Milei then quoted Alberto Benegas-Lynch's definition of classical liberalism, which he said would be his guiding philosophy: "Liberalism is the full respect for the life project of others, based on the principle of non-aggression, in defense of the right to life, liberty, and property, whose basic institutions are private property, markets free of government intervention, free competition, division of labor and social cooperation."[5]

Milei made good on his promises.

He slashed government spending.

He cut government departments.

As he told me, "We need to embrace the values of freedom, which are ideas in the United States—even though in recent times they may have been degraded and some might have walked off the path." And as he told the coddled Scavengers of Davos, "Economic freedom, limited government and unlimited respect for private property are essential elements for economic growth. The impoverishment produced by collectivism is not a fantasy, nor is it an inescapable fate. It's a reality that we Argentines know very well."[6]

When I meet him in the Casa Rosada, the building is largely empty.

The wood and marble chambers seem to echo with the silence of *ressentiment* that for a century characterized the governance of the country.

And then President Milei meets me in his office.

On the center of his enormous meeting table is a golden chain saw.

In our conversation, he cites the values of the Bible, the economics of Hayek.

The Lions are indeed awakening.

JERUSALEM, ISRAEL

I am in Jerusalem again.

I'm speaking at an event with my friend Douglas Murray, to be attended by some three thousand Israelis.

The mood in the country has changed.

When last I visited, some months ago, the mood was bleak. The Israeli war against Hamas was perhaps the most criticized military action in modern history, despite the fact that it was also the most precise operation in history. Anti-Semitism spiked around the world; Israelis found themselves targeted in the press, by foreign governments, by terrorism. Meanwhile, the Iranian government still threatened brutal military action; so did the best-armed terrorist group in the region, Hezbollah, on Israel's northern border in Lebanon.

Then something happened: Israel unsheathed its claws.

On July 13, 2024, Israel killed the head of Hamas's military wing, Mohammed Deif.

On July 31, Israel assassinated Hamas political leader Ismail Haniyeh in Tehran.

On September 17, Israel activated bombs inside the pagers of thousands of members of the Lebanese terrorist group Hezbollah, killing dozens and wounding thousands; a day later, Israel blew up their walkie-talkies and other communications devices. Just a few days after that, Israel launched a massive aerial assault on Hezbollah weapons caches, followed by a ground invasion. Within weeks, Israel had secured the entirety of southern Lebanon, forcing a cease-fire.

On October 16, Israel killed Hamas leader Yahya Sinwar, the October 7th mastermind.

On October 26, Israel launched a series of strikes on Iran that destroyed its air defense capabilities.

On this day in Jerusalem, the mood is different.

Israelis have roared.

The sacrifice they have undergone is extraordinary. During my speech, I ask members of the audience who have served during the war to stand; a quarter of the them do. Then I ask anyone with a family member who has served to stand. The entire audience stands.

They are not bowed. They are not broken.

They stand in pride.

Before the event, at the VIP reception, I am momentarily taken aback when a young man greets me. I recognize his face, but can't place him.

It takes me a moment before I realize who it is.

It is the twenty-one-year-old Israeli soldier who lost both legs and one of his arms.

The last time I saw him, he was in his motorized wheelchair.

This time he is standing.

He is wearing prosthetics; a broad smile creases his face.

He shakes my hand, thanks me for coming to the event.

I nod, pose for a picture.

And then he walks away.

Walks.

Israel exists in a region of Scavengers. The Scavengers never sleep. They have allies around the world: in the press, in the universities, in governments.

But neither do the Lions.

The Lions are awake.

WASHINGTON, DC

The nation's capital is freezing.

But the sun is out.

Today is the day.

At 7:45 a.m., we start walking from the Marriott hotel toward the set, which overlooks the National Mall and the US Capitol. The inauguration of Donald J. Trump as forty-seventh president of the United States was originally slated to take place outside, but the temperature has dropped precipitously, and so amid rumors of security concerns, the entire event has been moved inside the Capitol Building. We had invites, but we're covering the event live instead.

The walk is beautiful—the mood that pervades the capital is one of excitement. People stop me on the street for photos, smiling brightly despite the brutal chill. I do my show, looking forward to the inauguration, and then the rest of the *Daily Wire Backstage* cast joins me—Jeremy Boreing, Matt Walsh, Andrew Klavan, Michael Knowles.

The temperature begins to warm a bit.

On our screens, we watch as the highest-ranking members of the American government enter the Capitol Rotunda. Religious figures from a variety of faiths offer prayers for the new administration.

Beneath *The Apotheosis of Washington*, President Trump is sworn into office by Chief Justice John Roberts.

Behind us, in the park, cannons boom repeatedly, signaling Trump's accession. We can see their smoke rising through the trees.

Jubilance.

Something new is beginning.

As Trump speaks, he is flanked by the failed Scavengers of the past, but also by the leaders of American innovation. He pledges himself to a "golden era" and vows, "We will forge a society that is colorblind and merit-based . . . we will begin the complete restoration of America and the revolution of common sense."

He concludes:

We will be prosperous, we will be proud, we will be strong, and we will win like never before. We will not be conquered, we will not be intimidated, we will not be broken, and we will not fail. From this day on, the United States of America will be a free, sovereign, and independent nation. We will stand bravely, we will live proudly, we will dream boldly, and nothing will stand in our way because we are Americans. The future is ours, and our golden age has just begun.

Then Carrie Underwood is ushered forward to sing "America the Beautiful."

And the audio cuts out.

There are a few moments of confusion—then Underwood does something terrific. She says, "I can just sing it," and begins to sing the great standard on her own. The crowd—Democrats and Republicans alike—join in.

From sea to shining sea . . .

Then the ceremony is over.

President Trump and Vice President JD Vance usher the former president, Joe Biden, to a waiting helicopter, to take them to their new life, no longer in control of the levers of American government. From our vantage we can see clearly as the helicopter lifts off, leaving behind a dark time of envy and ugliness.

It's warmer now as we prepare to close our broadcast.

Perhaps the new administration will keep its promises. Perhaps not. Politics, after all, is a brutal and difficult game.

But something has changed.

Americans have changed.

The 2024 election was a sign that a new day is indeed dawning.

The Lions are awake again.

It is sometimes difficult to find solutions to long-standing, intractable problems.

Prescriptions fail to do justice to the magnitude of those problems, fail to specify in enough detail or nuance just what must be done.

That is not so in the battle between the Lions and the Scavengers.

For the Lions to win requires no great scheme, no clever machinations.

It requires just one thing: courage.

It requires the Lion to roar.

When the Pride stands, the Pack falls away.

When the Lion stands, the Scavenger flees.

It is not enough for the Lion to stand.

He must pass on his wisdom.

The Lion must believe and preach the power of a cognizable, God-driven universe; must teach his cubs that they are made in the image of God, with the power to choose; that moral meaningful duties exist in the world, and that we must fulfill them. The Lion must not be shy in inculcating these lessons in his young—there is no such thing as a vacuum in values, and any gap left by the Lion will be filled by the envy and cruelty of the Scavenger. The Lions must actively reward and celebrate the hunter; support and cheer the warrior; protect and cherish the weaver.

The Lion must protect free minds and free markets, public virtue and equal rights under law.

The Lion must brush away his masochistic, narcissistic guilt.

The Lion must reembrace himself.

The Lion must unsheathe his own claws, and pass on his ways to the next generation. For civilization is always one generation away from falling to the predations of the Scavenger.

And what of the Scavengers?

The Scavengers will never go away, for in each human heart, the battle between Lion and Scavenger rages. Sin crouches at all of our doors, but we can master it. If we are faced with challenges, we must first seek the answer in ourselves, not in our stars; we must deny the Great Conspiracy Theory in favor of the logic of God, as stated in Deuteronomy: "This day I call the heavens and the earth as witnesses against you that I have set before you life and death, blessings and curses. Now choose life, so that you and your children may live."[7]

We must not become creatures of envy.

And we must deny the creatures of envy the ammunition of our unearned shame.

The Scavengers will never surrender.

The battle will go on for the rest of time.

But they cannot win.

Unless we let them.

When I began writing this book, the Scavengers had the upper hand.

The Lions were weary.

They lay in the dust, weary and wounded.

The Scavengers circled, sniffing blood.

Now the Lion stands again.

All the Lions awaken.

The Pride is returning.

And the Scavengers should tremble.

ACKNOWLEDGMENTS

Some books are suffused with a cold objectivity. Others are written at white heat. This book was written passionately, because we live in shockingly turbulent times, and because the truth has never been more urgently necessary. This book is also the culmination of years of travel and learning and involvement in the fight—none of which would be possible without all the business partners, staff, supporters, friends and family who stand beside me.

First and foremost, I must thank our audience. That audience has been there, growing and listening and giving us feedback, every day for decades. Their dedication, stalwartness, and constant support is a buttress for all of us in waging what we believe to be an important civilizational battle—we're privileged to be able to speak to them, and often, to voice the opinions they want heard in the public square. It's a privilege to speak to you every day, and an even greater privilege to be entrusted with your time and, I hope, your cause.

I must also thank my business partners and our investors at the Daily Wire, a company founded by me, Jeremy Boreing, and Caleb Robinson a decade ago. When we started the company, it was just a few of us operating from Jeremy's poolhouse. It's now grown to become a media powerhouse on the right—and that's due to the brilliance and dedication of my business partners. What we've built wouldn't be possible without the amazing employees of our chaotic and bustling enterprise, who have to adjust minute-to-minute to our wildest ideas and the most insane news cycles. Here, I would be remiss if I didn't single out my executive assistant, Kelly, who ensures that my life runs on time (or, for that matter, at all), as well as my executive producer, Justin, and all the production staff, who collectively make it possible for me to deliver my show on a daily basis.

A big thank you goes to Keith Urbahn, my agent at Javelin, who was willing to take me on as a client. I've had agents at other big agencies—and you'll be unsurprised to learn that those agencies were less than willing to take me on as a client again given the polarization of our politics. Keith didn't hesitate for a single second. No one could ask for a better advocate.

My gratitude goes also to the amazing editors at Simon & Schuster, who have been unstinting in their wisdom and enthusiasm: to Jonathan Karp and Jen Bergstrom for being steadfast defenders of the First Amendment and seeing the potential in this book; Natasha Simons for her superb editorial advice; and Jen Long, Jennifer Robinson, Clara Linhoff, and Tom Spain for their hard work. I look forward to working together on many projects to come.

My thanks also to the team at Singer Burke as well as Michael Sherman, who always look out for my interests and act as an advocate for them—even when I do a less-than-stellar job of that myself.

Living a public life can be difficult—privacy isn't exactly a commodity in large supply. That means that as my wife and I raise our children, our local religious Jewish community is a vital part of our life. An enormous and undying thank you to all the members of that community, our friends and our colleagues, who help keep us grounded and protect our children from the vicissitudes of that public life. In particular, thank you to the Kidron family, our great friends, who share with us both the wonderful and difficult times in our lives.

And then there is our family.

Thank you to my in-laws, who are always there to offer some well-timed advice as well as play with our kids; to all of my kids' cousins and their parents, who make our lives rich with meaning and joy; and to my parents, who have been my moral examplars my entire life, and who remain the most reliable and generous people I know.

Thank you to my children, who ensure that no matter how grave things get in the world, that our life is a constant adventure, filled with delight and annoyance and hilarity and chaotic beauty.

Thank you to my wife, who remains the best person I know—the warm, beating heart of my life, who knows that in the end, no matter what I say or do, my role as a husband and a father is the most important job I will ever do. Thank you for your generosity, your caring, and your love. You never know what kind of person you're marrying when you sign up for a life commitment, and that's particularly true when you're both young. You take a leap of faith.

Best leap ever.

And finally, thanks to God, who gave me the gift of life, all the things any man could ask for, and most of all, the opportunity to fulfill my potential by using my voice in His defense.

NOTES

INTRODUCTION

1. https://x.com/najmamsharif/status/1710689657757769783?s=20.
2. J. R. R. Tolkien, *The Return of the King* (HarperCollins ebooks), 1075.
3. Proverbs 29:18.
4. C. S. Lewis, *The Screwtape Letters* (HarperCollins, 2001), 161.
5. Seneca, *On Anger*, in *Moral and Political Essays* (Cambridge University Press, 1995), 70.
6. John Milton, *Paradise Lost*, I 258–63.
7. Mao Zedong, *Speech at the Sixth Plenum of the Sixth Central Committee of the Communist Party of China* (1938).
8. As quoted in Alvaro Vargas Llosa, "The Killing Machine," Independent Institute, July 11, 2005, https://www.independent.org/news/article.asp?id=1535
9. Rudyard Kipling, "Recessional" (1897), www.poetryfoundation.org/poems/46780/recessional.

CHAPTER ONE: THE WAY OF THE LION

1. Homer, *The Iliad*, trans. Robert Fagles (Penguin Classics, 1990), Book 24: 613–14.
2. Sir Isaac Newton, *Natural Philosophy*, trans. Andrew Motte (Daniel Adee: 1848), 504.
3. Deuteronomy 30:15–19.
4. Thomas Sowell, *Knowledge and Decisions* (Basic Books, 1996), xiv.
5. Ibid, 5.
6. F. A. Hayek, *The Constitution of Liberty* (University of Chicago Press, 2011), 78.
7. Rudyard Kipling, "The Glory of the Garden," in *The Islanders*, in *Kipling Poems* (Everyman's Library Pocket Poets, 2007), 184.

NOTES

CHAPTER TWO: THE PRIDE

1. Rudyard Kipling, "The Law of the Jungle," in *Kipling Poems* (Everyman's Library Pocket Poets, 2007), 74.
2. Marcus Aurelius, *The Wisdom of Marcus Aurelius*, trans. George Long (Murat Durmus, 2023).
3. Robert M. Pirsig, *Zen and the Art of Motorcycle Maintenance* (Bantam Books, 1981), 350.
4. Jim Collins, *Good to Great* (HarperCollins, 2001).
5. David McCullough, *The Pioneers* (Simon & Schuster, 2019), 258.
6. Alexis de Tocqueville, *Democracy in America*, trans. Henry Reeve, https://www.gutenberg.org/files/816/816-h/816-h.htm.
7. Ayn Rand, *Capitalism: The Unknown Ideal* (Penguin, 1986), 22.
8. Walter Isaacson, *Musk* (Simon & Schuster, 2023), 442.
9. Steve Jobs, Stanford University Commencement Address, 2005, https://www.youtube.com/watch?v=UF8uR6Z6KLc.
10. LendingTree Analysis of Bureau of Labor Statistics, https://www.lendingtree.com/business/small/failure-rate/.
11. Victor Davis Hanson, *Carnage and Culture: Landmark Battles in the Rise of Western Power* (First Anchor Books, 2001), 7.
12. Congressman Steve Israel, ed., *Charge! History's Greatest Military Speeches* (Naval Institute Press, 2007), 13.
13. Abraham Lincoln, Remarks to the 166th Ohio Regiment, August 22, 1864, https://housedivided.dickinson.edu/sites/lincoln/speech-to-166th-ohio-regiment-august-22-1864/.
14. George Patton, Speech to the Third Army, May 31, 1944.
15. Hanson, *Carnage and Culture*, 365.
16. Gil Troy, *The Zionist Ideas* (Jewish Publication Society, 2018).
17. William Tecumseh Sherman, *Memoirs* (Penguin, 2000), 495.
18. Geoffrey Blainey, *The Causes of War* (Free Press, 1988), 53.
19. George Eliot, *Middlemarch* (Modernista, 2024).
20. St. Thomas Aquinas, *Summa Theologica* (E-artnow, 2013).
21. Matthew 7:25.
22. Russell Kirk, *The Politics of Prudence* (Intercollegiate Studies Institute, 2014).
23. Exodus 34:6.
24. Tractate *Nedarim* 39b.
25. William Shakespeare, *The Merchant of Venice*, Act IV, Scene I.
26. Isaiah 49:15.
27. Proverbs 31:26–31.
28. William Shakespeare, Sonnet 116.
29. Ezekiel 19:2.
30. Genesis 17:4–14.
31. Genesis 2:18.
32. Edmund Burke, *Reflections on the Revolution in France* (Penguin Books, 1982).

NOTES

CHAPTER THREE: THE RULES OF THE PRIDE

1. "Apotheosis of Washington," AOC.gov, https://www.aoc.gov/explore-capitol-campus/art/apotheosis-washington.
2. Karlyn Barker, "He Painted America's Story," *Washington Post*, February 25, 2004, https://www.washingtonpost.com/archive/local/2004/02/26/he-painted-americas-story/b4b8a163-0b11-46f5-bf56-841db56ec67c/.
3. Alexis de Tocqueville, *Democracy in America*, trans. Delbs Winthrop and Harvey Mansfield (University of Chicago Press, 2012), 388.
4. John Adams, *Defence of the Constitutions of Government of the United States* (1787), https://press-pubs.uchicago.edu/founders/documents/v1ch15s34.html.
5. Thomas Jefferson to John Adams, October 28, 1813, https://press-pubs.uchicago.edu/founders/documents/v1ch15s61.html.
6. Isaiah Berlin, *Liberty* (Oxford University Press, 2017), 222–23.
7. St. Thomas Aquinas, *Summa Theologica*, Question 10, Article 8, https://www.newadvent.org/summa/3010.htm#article8.
8. Thomas Jefferson, Virginia Statute on Religious Freedom (1786), https://virginiahistory.org/learn/thomas-jefferson-and-virginia-statute-religious-freedom.
9. F. A. Hayek, *The Constitution of Liberty* (University of Chicago Press, 2011), 74.
10. Robert Michael Citino, *The German Way of War: From the Thirty Years War to the Third Reich* (University Press of Kansas, 2005); Edwin Luttwak, *Strategy: The Logic of War and Peace* (Harvard University Press, 2001).
11. Jocko Willink and Leif Babin, *Extreme Ownership: How US Navy SEALs Lead and Win* (St. Martin's, 2015), 176.
12. Edwin Luttwak, *The Art of Military Innovation* (Harvard University Press, 2023), 4.
13. Daron Acemoglu and James A. Robinson, *Why Nations Fail* (Crown Business, 2012), 74.
14. John Locke, *Second Treatise* (1689), §27.
15. Richard Pipes, *Property and Freedom* (Vintage Books, 1999), 76.
16. Nicholaus S. Noles and Susan A. Gelman, "You Can't Always Want What You Get: Children's Intuitions About Ownership and Desire," *Cognitive Development* 31 (July 2014): 59–68.
17. Thomas Sowell, "The Quest for Cosmic Justice," Hoover Institution, January 30, 2000, https://www.hoover.org/research/quest-cosmic-justice.
18. Kurt Vonnegut, "Harrison Bergeron" (1961), https://archive.org/stream/HarrisonBergeron/Harrison%20Bergeron_djvu.txt.
19. Adam Smith, *Lectures on Justice, Police, Revenue and Arms* (Clarendon Press, 1896), 253.
20. Hayek, *The Constitution of Liberty*, 207.
21. Mark Lieberman, "Average Teacher Pay Passes $70K. How Much Is It in Your State?," *Education Week*, May 7, 2024, https://www.edweek.org/teaching-learning/average-teacher-pay-passes-70k-how-much-is-it-in-your-state/2024/05.

22. Katherine Schaeffer, "Key Facts About Public School Teachers in the U.S.," Pew Research Center, September 24, 2024, https://www.pewresearch.org/short-reads/2024/09/24/key-facts-about-public-school-teachers-in-the-u-s/.
23. Joseph Schumpeter, *The Theory of Economic Development*, trans. Redvers Opie (1934).
24. Walter Isaacson, *Innovators* (Simon & Schuster, 2015), 1.
25. Friedrich A. Hayek, "The Uses of Knowledge in Society," https://www.econlib.org/library/Essays/hykKnw.html.
26. Schumpeter, *The Theory of Economic Development*.
27. Leonard Read, "I Pencil: My Family Tree," December 1958, https://oll.libertyfund.org/titles/read-i-pencil-my-family-tree-as-told-to-leonard-e-read-dec-1958.
28. Bernie Sanders, *It's Okay to Be Angry About Capitalism* (Crown, 2023), 164.
29. "Nine Charts Which Tell You All You Need to Know About North Korea," BBC, September 26, 2017, https://www.bbc.com/news/world-asia-41228181.
30. John Kingston, "HumanProgress.org Founder: Time Is Money, and We're All Getting Richer," *Freight Waves*, June 21, 2023, https://finance.yahoo.com/news/humanprogress-org-founder-time-money-202500571.html.
31. Marian L. Tupy, "The Great Miracle of Industrialization," Human Progress, May 6, 2019, https://humanprogress.org/the-miracle-of-industrialization/.
32. Adam Smith, *The Theory of Moral Sentiments* (1759), https://oll.libertyfund.org/titles/smith-the-theory-of-moral-sentiments-and-on-the-origins-of-languages-stewart-ed.
33. John D. Rockefeller, *John D. Rockefeller on Making Money* (Skyhorse, 2015).
34. Robert Nisbet, *The Twilight of Authority* (Liberty Fund, 2022), 232–33.
35. Alexis de Tocqueville, "On the Use That the Americans Make of Association in Civil Life," from *Democracy in America*, trans. Harvey Mansfield and Delba Winthrop, http://www.press.uchicago.edu/Misc/Chicago/805328.html.
36. Alisdaire MacIntyre, *After Virtue: A Study in Moral Theory* (University of Notre Dame Press, 2007), 263.
37. Hernando de Soto, *The Mystery of Capital* (Basic Books, 2000), 16, 47.
38. James Madison, *Federalist* No. 51 (1788), https://avalon.law.yale.edu/18th_century/fed51.asp.
39. Daron Acemoglu and James A. Robinson, *Why Nations Fail* (Crown Business, 2012), 208.
40. Ayn Rand, *Capitalism: The Unknown Ideal* (Penguin, 1986), 150.

CHAPTER FOUR: THE WAY OF THE SCAVENGER

1. "Famous Oxonians," University of Oxford, https://www.ox.ac.uk/about/oxford-people/famous-oxonians.
2. "Sir Launcelot's Vision of the Sanc Grael," Rossetti Archive, rossettiarchive.org/docs/s93.raw.html.
3. Adam Smith, *The Theory of Moral Sentiments* (1759), https://oll.libertyfund.org/titles/smith-the-theory-of-moral-sentiments-and-on-the-origins-of-languages-stewart-ed.

NOTES

4. Friedrich Nietzsche, *On the Genealogy of Morality* (Cambridge University Press, 2006), 17.
5. Karl Marx, *Marx on Religion*, ed. John C. Raines (Temple University Press, 2002).
6. Alan Hunt and Gary Wickham, *Foucault and Law* (Pluto Press, 1994), 15–16.
7. Friedrich Nietzsche, *Beyond Good and Evil* (Knopf, 2010), 203.
8. Jean-Paul Sartre, *Essays in Existentialism* (Citadel Press, 1993), 41.
9. John Milton, *Paradise Lost*, IX 703–5.
10. Percy Bysshe Shelley, in Raymond Macdonald Alden, ed., *Critical Essays of the Early Nineteenth Century* (Scribner's, 1921), 298.
11. Robin DiAngelo, *White Fragility* (Beacon Press, 2018), 17.
12. Charles Perragin, "'Meritocracy Will Never Be a Fair Ideal': Interview with Michael Sandel," Philonemist, September 29, 2021, https://www.philonomist.com/en/interview/meritocracy-will-never-be-fair-ideal.
13. Jeremy Olshan, "Meritocracy Isn't an Alternative to Inequality—It's a Justification, Says This Harvard Philosopher," *MarketWatch*, December 21, 2020, https://www.marketwatch.com/story/meritocracy-isnt-an-alternative-to-inequality-its-a-justification-says-this-harvard-philosopher-11608334819.
14. John Rawls, *A Theory of Justice* (Oxford University Press, 1999).
15. Thomas Sowell, *Discrimination and Disparities* (Basic Books, 2019).
16. Karl Popper, *The Open Society and Its Enemies* (Taylor & Francis, 2012), 353.
17. Dan McLaughlin, "Nikole Hannah-Jones Responds to Our 1619 and Slavery Issue," *National Review*, February 8, 2022, https://www.nationalreview.com/corner/nikole-hannah-jones-responds-to-our-1619-and-slavery-issue/.
18. Alisdaire MacIntyre, *After Virtue: A Study in Moral Theory* (University of Notre Dame Press, 2007), 11–12.
19. MacIntyre, 23.
20. Ernesto Londano and Amy Julia Harris, "UnitedHealthcare CEO Laid to Rest as Family Mourns Privately," *New York Times*, December 11, 2024.
21. Chandler Dandridge, "Bernie Sanders: A Mass Movement Can Beat Health CEO Greed," *Jacobin*, December 11, 2024, https://jacobin.com/2024/12/sanders-movement-health-care-mangione.
22. Popper, *The Open Society and Its Enemies*, 353.
23. T. S. Eliot, *The Waste Land* (1922), www.poetryfoundation.org/poems/47311/the-waste-land.

CHAPTER FIVE: THE PACK

1. Jeremy W. Peters, "It's Not Just Gaza: Student Protesters See Links to a Global Struggle," *New York Times*, May 1, 2024, https://www.nytimes.com/2024/05/01/us/pro-palestinian-college-protests.html.
2. Karl Marx, *Capital: A Critique of Political Economy*, vol. I, https://www.marxists.org/archive/marx/works/1867-c1/.
3. Karl Marx and Freidrich Engels, *The Communist Manifesto* (Haymarket Books, 2005).

NOTES

4. V. I. Lenin, "The Revolutionary Proletariat and the Right of Nations to Self-Determination" (1915), https://www.marxists.org/archive/lenin/works/1915/oct/16.htm.
5. V. I. Lenin, "A Contribution to the History of the Question of the Dictatorship" (1920), https://www.marxists.org/archive/lenin/works/1920/oct/20.htm#fw04.
6. Vladimir Lenin to the Bolsheviks of Penza, August 11, 1918, as quoted in Simon Sebag Montefiore, *Written in History: Letters That Changed the World* (Knopf, 2019).
7. Richard Pipes, *The Russian Revolution* (Vintage Books, 1990), 820.
8. Timothy Snyder, *Bloodlands* (Basic Books, 2011).
9. Jean-Jacques Rousseau, *A Discourse Upon the Origin and the Foundation of the Inequality Among Mankind* (1755), https://www.gutenberg.org/cache/epub/11136/pg11136-images.html.
10. Slavoj Zizek, "The Game of Life," iai player, https://iai.tv/video/the-game-of-life.
11. Slavoj Zizek, "Robespierre or the 'Divine Terror' of Violence," Lacan.com, https://www.lacan.com/zizrobes.htm.
12. Ayn Rand, *Atlas Shrugged* (Plume, 2003).
13. Cornelius Tacitus, *The Annals*, ed. Alfred John Church and William Jackson Brodribb, 15.37, https://www.perseus.tufts.edu/hopper/text?doc=Perseus%3Atext%3A1999.02.0078%3Abook%3D15%3Achapter%3D37.
14. Tacitus, *The Histories* (I.4), https://en.wikisource.org/wiki/The_Histories_(Tacitus)/Book_1#4.
15. 1 Corinthians 6:18–20 (English Standard Version).
16. Carl Trueman, *The Rise and Triumph of the Modern Self* (Crossway, 2020), 43.
17. Trueman, 63.
18. Marquis de Sade, *120 Days of Sodom* (Start Publishing, 2013).
19. Betsey Stevenson and Justin Wolfers, "The Paradox of Declining Female Happiness," *American Economic Journal: Economic Policy* 1, no. 2 (2009): 190–225, https://journalistsresource.org/wp-content/uploads/2013/01/WomensHappiness.pdf.
20. Tom Acres, "Google Reveals What We Searched for the Most in 2023," Sky News, December 11, 2023, https://news.sky.com/story/google-reveals-what-we-searched-for-the-most-in-2023-13028024.
21. Chandrasekaran.
22. Rudyard Kipling, "A Pict Song," in *The Islanders*, in *Kipling Poems* (Everyman's Library Pocket Poets, 2007), 155.
23. Frantz Fanon, *The Wretched of the Earth* (Grove Press, 1963), 35–36.
24. Ibid, 39–40.
25. Ibid, 36.
26. Ibid, 43.
27. Jean-Paul Sartre, Preface to Fanon, *The Wretched of the Earth*, 22.
28. Ibid, 25–26.
29. Ibid, 29.

NOTES

30. Joshua Muravchik, "Enough Said: The False Scholarship of Edward Said," *World Affairs Journal*, April 1, 2013, https://www.meforum.org/campus-watch/enough-said-the-false-scholarship-of-edward-said.
31. Edward W. Said, *Orientalism* (Vintage Books, 1979), 3.
32. Muravchik, "Enough Said."
33. Edward W. Said, *The Question of Palestine* (Vintage Books, 1979), 184.
34. Said, *The Question of Palestine*, 75.
35. Ta-Nehisi Coates, *Between the World and Me* (Random House, 2015), 143.
36. Coates, 111.
37. Ta-Nehisi Coates, *The Message* (Diversified, 2024), 128.
38. Edward Said, "Islam and the West Are Inadequate Banners," *Guardian*, September 16, 2001, https://www.theguardian.com/world/2001/sep/16/september11.terrorism3.
39. Coates, *Between the World and Me*, 87.
40. https://x.com/realchrisrufo/status/1716593360973209998/photo/2.
41. Eric Hoffer, *The True Believer* (Harper & Row, 1951), 29–30.
42. Hoffer, 40.
43. Mary Matossian, "Ideologies of Delayed Industrialization: Some Tensions and Ambiguities," *Economic Development and Cultural Change* 6, no. 3 (April 1958), https://www.journals.uchicago.edu/doi/10.1086/449767.
44. Gary Saul Morson, "Falling in Love with Terror," *New York Review of Books*, January 13, 2022, https://www.nybooks.com/articles/2022/01/13/falling-in-love-with-terror/.
45. Barton Swaim, "Violent Protest and the Intelligentsia," *Wall Street Journal*, June 5, 2020, https://www.wsj.com/articles/violent-protest-and-the-intelligentsia-11591400422.
46. Gary Saul Morson, "Re-Possessed," *Commentary*, October 2024, https://www.commentary.org/articles/gary-morson/dostoevsky-depicts-woke-totalitarianism/.
47. Morson, "Falling in Love with Terror."
48. Jordan Moss and Peter J. O'Connor, "The Dark Triad Traits Predict Authoritarian Political Correctness and Alt-right Attitudes," *Heliyon* 6, no. 7 (July 2020): e04453, https://pmc.ncbi.nlm.nih.gov/articles/PMC7369609/.
49. William Shakespeare, *Coriolanus*, Act III, Scene 1 (ll. 121–27).

CHAPTER SIX: THE RULES OF THE PACK

1. Adolf Hitler, *Mein Kampf* (True Sign, 2023), 294.
2. Karl Marx, letter to Sigfrid Meyer and August Vogt in New York, April 9, 1870, https://www.marxists.org/archive/marx/works/1870/letters/70_04_09.htm.
3. Freidrich Engels, letter to Franz Mehring, July 14, 1893, https://www.marxists.org/archive/marx/works/1893/letters/93_07_14.htm.
4. Vladimir Ilyich Lenin, *What Is to Be Done?* (1901), trans. Joe Fineberg and George Hanna, https://www.marxists.org/archive/lenin/works/1901/witbd/ii.htm.

5. Ron Eyerman, "False Consciousness and Ideology in Marxist Theory," *Acta Sociologica* 24, no. 1–2 (1981): 43–56, https://www.jstor.org/stable/4194332?read-now=1&seq=1#page_scan_tab_contents.
6. Simone de Beauvoir, *The Second Sex* (Vintage Books, 2010), 9–10.
7. Herbert Marcuse, *Eros and Civilization* (Beacon Press, 1974), 5.
8. Frantz Fanon, *The Wretched of the Earth* (Grove Press, 1963), 56.
9. Jean-Paul Sartre, *Preface* in Fanon, 13
10. Robert Conquest, "The Human Cost of Soviet Communism," Testimony before the Subcommittee to Investigate the Administration of the Internal Security Act and Other Internal Security Laws, 91st Congress, 2nd Session (US Government Printing Office, 1970), 19.
11. Conquest, 27.
12. Betty Friedan, *It Changed My Life* (Harvard University Press, 1998), 397.
13. Edward W. Said, *The Question of Palestine* (Vintage Books, 1979), 88.
14. George Gilder, *Knowledge and Power* (Skyhorse, 2013), 4.
15. Eric Hoffer, *The True Believer* (Harper & Row: 1951), 41.
16. President Lyndon Baines Johnson, Commencement Address at Howard University, June 4, 1965, https://www.presidency.ucsb.edu/documents/commencement-address-howard-university-fulfill-these-rights.
17. Bailey Peraita, "The $1,500 Sandwich-from-Scratch Guy: 'Now It's Hard for Me to Waste Any Food,'" *Guardian*, September 23, 2015, https://www.theguardian.com/lifeandstyle/2015/sep/23/1500-sandwich-from-scratch-andy-george-youtube-food-supply-chain.
18. Yanis Varoufakis, *Talking to My Daughter About Capitalism* (Farrar, Straus & Giroux, 2018), 30.
19. Karl Marx, "The German Ideology" (1845), https://www.marxists.org/archive/marx/works/1845/german-ideology/ch01a.htm.
20. Peter Singer, "Why We Must Ration Health Care," *New York Times*, July 15, 2009, https://www.nytimes.com/2009/07/19/magazine/19healthcare-t.html.
21. Thomas Sowell, *Basic Economics: A Common Sense Guide to the Economy* (Basic Books, 2015).
22. Bernie Sanders, *It's Okay to Be Angry About Capitalism* (Crown, 2023), 98.
23. Tucker Carlson, Fox News, January 2, 2019.
24. Benito Mussolini, "The Doctrine of Fascism" (1932), https://sjsu.edu/faculty/wooda/2B-HUM/Readings/The-Doctrine-of-Fascism.pdf.
25. Sanders, *It's Okay to Be Angry About Capitalism*, 263.
26. Karl Marx and Freidrich Engels, *The Communist Manifesto* (Haymarket Books, 2005).
27. "Questions & Answers to American Trade Unionists: Stalin's Interview with the First American Trade Union Delegation to Soviet Russia," *Pravda*, September 15, 1927, https://www.marxists.org/reference/archive/stalin/works/1927/09/15.htm.
28. Yuri Druzhnikov, *Informer 001: The Myth of Pavlik Morozov* (Transaction, 2012), 103.
29. San Francisco Gay Men's Chorus, "Creating Change Through Music," https://www.sfgmc.org/mission.

NOTES

30. https://www.youtube.com/watch?v=YW6p6z7yYlY.
31. Christopher F. Rufo, "The Real Story Behind Drag Queen Story Hour," *City Journal*, Autumn 2022, https://www.city-journal.org/article/the-real-story-behind-drag-queen-story-hour.
32. Wilhelm Reich, *The Mass Psychology of Fascism* (1933), https://archive.org/stream/MassPsychologyOfFascism-WilhelmReich/mass-psychology-reich_djvu.txt.
33. Christina Hoff Sommers, "Reconsiderations: Betty Friedan's 'The Feminine Mystique,'" *New York Sun*, September 17, 2008, https://www.nysun.com/arts/reconsiderations-betty-friedans-the-feminine/86003/.
34. Shulamith Firestone, *The Dialectic of Sex* (Women's Press, 1979), https://www.marxists.org/subject/women/authors/firestone-shulamith/dialectic-sex.htm.
35. Frantz Fanon, *The Wretched of the Earth* (Grove Press, 1963), 42.
36. Edward W. Said, *Orientalism* (Vintage Books, 1979), 49.
37. Said, *Orientalism*, 100.
38. Ta-Nehisi Coates, *Between the World and Me* (Random House, 2015), 70.
39. Robert Nisbet, *Twilight of Authority* (Liberty Fund, 2022), 76.
40. Jon Miltimore, "Hayek: Social Justice Demands the Unequal Treatment of Individuals," Foundation for Economic Education, November 13, 2018, https://fee.org/articles/hayek-social-justice-demands-the-unequal-treatment-of-individuals/.
41. Amity Shlaes, *Great Society: A New History* (Harper, 2019), 98–99.
42. https://x.com/KamalaHarris/status/1322963321994289154?lang=en.
43. Ibram X. Kendi, *How to Be an Antiracist* (One World, 2019), 19.
44. Julie Buckler, "Lenin's Dacha: The Epitome of Political Prominence," in *The Urban Imagination*, exhibit, Harvard University, https://hum54-15.omeka.fas.harvard.edu/exhibits/show/russian_dacha/lenin-s-dacha--the-epitome-of-.
45. Vladimir Lenin, "The Proletarian Revolution and the Renegade Kautsky," https://www.marxists.org/archive/lenin/works/1918/prrk/common_liberal.htm.
46. Gary Saul Morson, "Faith and Russian Literature," *First Things*, May 2024, https://www.firstthings.com/article/2024/05/faith-and-russian-literature.
47. Arthur Koestler, *Darkness at Noon* (Macmillan, 1941).
48. Sanders, *It's Okay to Be Angry About Capitalism*, 263.
49. Kristine Phillips, "New York's Next Attorney General Targeted Slumlords. Now She's Going after Trump," *Washington Post*, December 19, 2018, https://www.washingtonpost.com/politics/2018/12/19/new-yorks-next-attorney-general-targeted-slumlords-now-shes-going-after-trump/.
50. Victor Klemperer, *I Will Bear Witness*, vol. 1, *1933–1941* (Random House, 1999), 224.
51. Norham H. Baynes, ed., *The Speeches of Adolf Hitler, 1922–1939* (Pennsylvania State University Press, 1942), 7.
52. "Adolf Hitler's Order of the Day Calling for Invasion of Yugoslavia and Greece," *New York Times*, April 7, 1941.

53. Gunter Riemann, *The Vampire Economy* (Vanguard Press, 1939), 6.
54. "The German Churches and the Nazi State," *Holocaust Encyclopedia*, https://encyclopedia.ushmm.org/content/en/article/the-german-churches-and-the-nazi-state.
55. Ian Kershaw, *Hitler 1936–1945: Nemesis* (Norton, 2000), 40.
56. Alan Bullock, *Hitler: A Study in Tyranny* (Odhams Press, 1952), 356.
57. Frank McDonough, *The Hitler Years: Triumph 1933–1939* (St. Martin's, 2019).
58. Mark Landler, "Results of Secret Nazi Breeding Program: Ordinary Folks," *New York Times*, November 7, 2006, https://www.nytimes.com/2006/11/07/world/europe/07nazi.html.
59. Felix Kersten, *The Kersten Memoirs 1940–1945* (Hutchinson, 1956), 176.
60. William Shirer, *Berlin Diary* (Rosetta Books, 1941).
61. William Shirer, *The Rise and Fall of the Third Reich* (Simon & Schuster, 1960), 268.
62. Adolf Hitler, Speech to the Reichstag Assuming New Power, April 26, 1942, Jewish Virtual Library, https://www.jewishvirtuallibrary.org/adolf-hitler-speech-to-the-reichstag-assuming-new-power-april-1942.

CHAPTER SEVEN: BLOODLUST AND BLOODGUILT

1. Soren Kierkegaard, *The Present Age* (Harper Torchbooks, 1962).
2. Vasily Grossman, *Life and Fate* (New York Review of Books, 2012), 840.
3. Ruth Benedict, *The Chrysanthemum and the Sword* (Houghton Mifflin, 1946).
4. Peter Salmon, "Jacques Derrida's Defense of Marx and the Birth of Hauntology," *Jacobin*, October 7, 2021, https://jacobin.com/2021/10/jacques-derrida-defense-of-marxism-hauntology-specters-of-marx-deconstruction-postmodernism-post-structuralism.
5. Pascal Bruckner, *The Tyranny of Guilt* (Princeton University Press, 2010), 3.
6. Shelby Steele, *White Guilt* (HarperCollins, 2006).
7. Bradford Betz, "Ocasio-Cortez Agrees That a World That Allows for Billionaires Is Immoral," Fox News, January 22, 2019, https://www.foxnews.com/politics/rep-alexandria-ocasio-cortez-agrees-a-world-that-allows-for-billionaires-is-immoral.
8. Thomas Sowell, "Apologizing for Civilization," in *Is Reality Optional?* (Hoover Institution Press, 2020).
9. Helmut Schoeck, *Envy: A Theory of Social Behavior* (Liberty Fund, 1987), 305.
10. Richard J. Evans, *The Third Reich in Power* (Penguin Books, 2005).
11. Niccolo Machiavelli, *The Works of the famous Nicholas Machiavel, citizen and secretary of Florence written originally in Italian, and from thence newly and faithfully translated into English* (London, 1680), https://quod.lib.umich.edu/e/eebo/A50274.0001.001/1:31.2.24?rgn=div3;view=fulltext.
12. Gilbert Chinard, *Thomas Jefferson, the Apostle of Americanism* (Good Press, 2019).
13. Abraham Lincoln, "July 4th Message to Congress," July 4, 1861, https://

millercenter.org/the-presidency/presidential-speeches/july-4-1861-july-4th-message-congress.
14. Noam Chomsky, *The Myth of American Idealism* (Penguin Press, 2024), 19–20.
15. Chomsky, 16.
16. "Current US Policies Toward China Are Outrageous: Noam Chomsky," *Global Times*, June 6, 2023, https://www.globaltimes.cn/page/202306/1292035.shtml.
17. Bruckner, *The Tyranny of Guilt*, 34.
18. *The Betrayed Girls* (BBC, 2017).
19. Pete Bainbridge, "Paedophile 'Daddy' Who Led Child Sex Grooming Ring in Rochdale Using Human Rights Laws to Try to Block Deportation," *Manchester Evening News*, February 17, 2016, https://www.manchestereveningnews.co.uk/news/greater-manchester-news/rochdale-grooming-gang-deportation-rights-10903124.
20. Salman Rushdie, *Joseph Anton* (Random House, 2012).
21. Jewish News Syndicate, "Iran's President Will Not Block Israel-Hamas Ceasefire amid Heavy Losses to Proxies," *New York Post*, January 15, 2025, https://nypost.com/2025/01/15/world-news/irans-president-will-not-block-israel-hamas-ceasefire-amid-heavy-losses-to-proxies/.
22. Luca Watson, "Ignore the Grooming Gangs Deniers," *The Critic*, January 16, 2025, https://thecritic.co.uk/ignore-the-grooming-gangs-deniers/.
23. Karl Popper, *The Open Society and Its Enemies* (Taylor & Francis, 2012), 340.
24. David Murrell, "Philly's New Generation of Unions Is Young, Progressive, and Coming to a Coffee Shop Near You," *Philadelphia*, October 17, 2020, https://www.phillymag.com/news/2020/10/17/philadelphia-unions/.
25. "Philadelphia: An Incomplete Revival," Center City District, Philadelphia, January 2017, https://centercityphila.org/uploads/attachments/ciyfyq8sr0mqsvlqdj6x1a8b3-ccr17-incompleterevival.pdf.

CHAPTER EIGHT: THE LION ROARS

1. Edward L. Glaeser, Rafael Di Tella, and Lucas Llach, "Introduction to Argentine Exceptionalism," *Latin American Economic Review* 27 (2018): 1, https://www.hbs.edu/ris/Publication%20Files/LAER%20Introduction%20to%20Argentine%20Exceptionalism_3c49e7ee-4f31-49a0-ba21-6c2b726cd7c5.pdf.
2. Luisa Rollenhagen, "Should a Notorious Buenos Aires Slum Become an Official Neighborhood?," *Guardian*, August 7, 2019, https://www.theguardian.com/cities/2019/aug/07/should-a-notorious-buenos-aires-slum-become-an-official-neighbourhood.
3. "Argentina Inflation Rate," Trading Economics, https://tradingeconomics.com/argentina/inflation-cpi#:~:text=Inflation%20Rate%20in%20Argentina%20averaged,de%20Estad%C3%ADstica%20y%20Censos%20(INDEC).
4. Jorge Luis Borges, "The Mountebank," in *Collected Ficciones of Jorge Luis Borges*, trans. Andrew Hurley (Penguin Press).

5. Javier Milei, Presidential Inaugural Address, December 10, 2023, https://www.americanrhetoric.com/speeches/javiermileipresidentialinauguraladdress.htm.
6. "Special Address by Javier Milei, President of Argentina," Davos 2024, World Economic Forum, January 18, 2024, https://www.weforum.org/stories/2024/01/special-address-by-javier-milei-president-of-argentina/.
7. Deuteronomy 30:19.